No Shit! There I Was... Series

NO SHIT!
THERE I WAS...
GONE WILD

By Michael Hodgson
Contributing Editor

Vol.3

ICS BOOKS, Inc. Merrillville, Indiana

Published by:
ICS BOOKS, Inc.
1370 E. 86th Place
Merrillville, IN 46410
800-541-7323

Co-Published in Canada by:
Vanwell Publishing LTD
1 Northrup Crescent
St. Catharines, Ontario
L2M 6P5
800-661-6136

All ICS titles are printed on 50% recycled paper from pre-consumer waste. All sheets are processed without using acid.

LIBRARY OF CONGRESS CATALOGING-IN-PUBLICATION DATA

No shit! There I was--gone wild / by Michael Hodgson, contributing editor
        p.   cm.
"Vol. 3'
ISBN 1-57034-041-2
1. Adventure and adventurers.   I. Hodgson, Michael .
G525.N543   1996   96-33998
910.4--dc20   CIP

Table of Contents

Introduction

Any outdoorsperson, armchair or otherwise, has learned that tall
tales are the stuff legends are made of, the meat of glory and the
marrow of adventure. For centuries, while gathered around campfires or smoky watering holes that smell of beer and musty wood,
adventurers the world over have regaled all who will listen in that
time honored tradition of recounting unbelievable stories that more
often than not begin with, "No shit! there I was...." or some other
reasonable facsimile. Exaggeration within moderation is key. Humor
becomes important, although not essential. Elements of the unbelievable are a must.

I must have heard nearly a million such stories during all the
years I have spent outdoors—both as a professional guide and an
outdoor writer. A number of these stories get handed down from storyteller to storyteller. An even greater number are pure originals,
gaining notoriety as much for the teller's art of verbally recounting
the event with humor and skill as for the event itself.

Truly great taletellers have the rare ability to make mountains out
of molehills if you give them half a chance. There is a craft in managing to embellish simple cowardice and elevate the tale to recounting an experience of inspiration, valor and glory. A mere sprained
ankle on a weekend backpack can turn into an epic event of biblical
proportions, bringing smiles and head shakes of disbelief from the
listeners when the lips of the skilled spinner of yarns crafts the tale.
Yet, too many of these narrations never get shared beyond the realm
of the campsite—disappearing come morning like the dying embers
of an evening's fire that once coaxed forth story after story.

It is with the above in mind that I set out to begin placing some of
these adventure narratives between the covers of a book for all to
enjoy—day in and day out. ICS Books and I created a writing contest, seeking the very best "No Shit! There I Was..." accounts the
outdoor world was willing to share. Stories arrived from all parts of
the country and before long, we had a best-selling anthology on our
hands. More stories kept arriving and the floodgates were open. No
Shit would become an annual writing contest, judged by professionals in the craft of writing and storytelling.

This third anthology in the highly popular *No Shit* series features the top 22 entries from 1995's contest which received hundreds of story entries from some amazingly skilled and entertaining liars, ahh, we mean writers, who specialize in weaving elements of believable and heroic fantasy from threads of outright stupidity and cowardice. *No Shit! There I Was...Gone Wild!* is a raconteur's finest feast, full of truly wild adventure tales that will leave you smiling, chuckling, chortling even screaming with glee. For obvious reasons, my two stories which are included in this book were not entered into the contest—had I won, could you imagine the scandal? That would be a *No Shit* story in itself.

My congratulations to this year's *No Shit* grand prize winner Marcus Woolf. Apparently, this is his first attempt at writing humor and I'm not amused—he's too damn funny for someone so young. I'll never be able to look at a frog without thinking of beer and margaritas again. Runner-up Rick Sanger only finished two judging points behind—the closest finish in our three young years of running this contest and a living testament to his story title—*Murphy Rules*. I am sure that everyone will have a favorite tale or two tucked between the pages within. I know I've got mine, and I read them over and over, as I am sure you will too.

In the meantime, maybe you've got a tale to tell? I hope so, because as you are reading this, ICS Books and I are already seeking and receiving more tales of unbelievable proportions for the next edition of this wonderfully entertaining collection of anthologies, *No Shit! There I Was...!*

Read on and enjoy. Then, if you do have a tale to share and think you have the right stuff to make it into these pages for storytelling posterity, read the contest criteria in the back of the book and send away for your official entry form.

Frogs and Hogs

By Marcus Woolf

Frogs Can't Survive in Margaritas—that was the headline on page 14 of the Calaveras County Frog Jumping Jubilee brochure. It sounded like a bar bet gone bad. I had come to Angels Camp, California, to spin a few simple words about the richest slices of Americana. You know...Mark Twain, the traditional county fair, apple pie, hot dogs. Liquored-up frogs didn't quite fit the bill. Of course, the article was referring to the fact that "salt and lime are poisonous to frogs, so they cannot live in sea water, limestone caves or margaritas." Yes, of course. How obvious. The three major environments where one is unlikely to find a croaking gaggle of frogs. It was an interesting claim, but wholly unfounded.

As an armchair scientist, I base my knowledge of the natural world on the Discovery Channel. Never have I seen a frog garnish the rim of a mixed drink. Nor have I seen those haughty National Geographic explorers chasing down a frog with a bottle of Cuervo and a handful of limes. No way was I going to believe the margarita maxim without following the scientific method. Of course, I hadn't taken the assignment to stir up trouble. But, from the article, I gathered that this wholesome affair might have its seedy side. At some point during this weekend extravaganza, someone was going to test this hypothesis, and I sure as heck was going to be there when it happened.

When I first entered the lush, rolling hills of Angels Camp, I thought there was no way a place of such beauty and warmth could be the laboratory for such an outlandish experiment. Tucked away in California's Gold Country, the small town appeared to be one of the last bastions of "family values." Young couples strolled their babies down the town's main street. Families on their way to the carnival cruised by in station wagons—smiling children hopping, froglike, up and down in the backseat in anticipation. I was none too happy about it. We'd need a little rougher crowd to actually stir up the guts to dunk a frog in liquor. But then again, frog jumping is not a completely innocent sport. It involves a healthy amount of scare tactics. These people were here to terrify frogs for kicks. There was hope.

1

Sanders, '96

Just when it was looking too pastoral, a massive horde of about 20 Harley Davidsons thundered in from a side street, with burly riders sporting ragged beards, dark shades and enough leather to scare a whole herd of cows. They were headed straight for our parade of families—*Easy Rider* meets *The Andy Griffith Show*. Now, what in the world were bikers doing in Angels Camp on frog day? Maybe they were here just to break up a good time. I thought about that old Marlon Brando movie, *The Wild Ones*, where the biker gang terrorizes the small town and takes over the local bar. Then I thought. Bikers...liquor...yes! All we needed was a frog. Things were looking up for my experiment.

The bikers revved their engines and exhaust pipes spewed noise, drowning out traffic. They were going to broadside the parade of families, and I gripped the steering wheel as "hog" enthusiast and frog enthusiast merged toward disaster.

No dice.

Ever so politely, the bikers merged with the station wagons. A biker waved thanks and slipped in front of an RV. No vulgar finger gestures, no shouting. The bikers joined the families and the happy little parade rolled right out of town—straight for the frog jubilee.

Gee gads, I wanted to puke. Bikers within reach of perhaps the world's largest frog population on Earth—the perfect recipe for a frog dunking, and someone had stripped the Hell out of Hell's Angels.

After I parked my car, I was waiting in line at the ticket window when a biker approached who was about 6 feet tall, with a plump face shrouded in a scraggly black beard and nothing but leather, grease and tattoos below that, like a vision of the apocalypse. Parents behind me gripped their children, and I hoped for trouble. Then, in a soft tone, he asked, "Is this where I can get my frog pin?"

"Huh?" I replied in as manly a voice as I could gulp out.

He tugged the right side of his leather vest and pointed to five tiny, tarnished frog buttons, right next to a pin of a Jack Daniels bottle. "I get one every year, and I usually get 'em here at this window."

"You gotta get 'em inside the fairgrounds this year," replied the lady behind the counter.

"Inside?" said the biker. He paused, ran his chubby index finger and thumb through his beard and hung his head. Don't deny a biker his frog pin, that's my motto. What if this man was a volcano ready to erupt? I sort of expected a fight to ensue. But without explanation, the disappointed biker merely turned and shuffled off. My image of bikers was crumbling.

I wanted to make a beeline to the first liquor stand to watch some first-class frog dunking. But I figured "frog jockey" would look great on my resume, so I headed for the Main Frog Jumping Stage. While I was going in with an open mind, what I saw disturbed me a little.

It was too quiet. Three large sets of bleachers were filled with an intense audience peering down at a huge stage. Craning their necks forward, elbows pressing into their knees, they studied the action in silence as one might study Barry Bonds at the plate. These people were taking this frog stuff way too seriously.

Each competitor placed a frog on a small red circle near the back of the stage. To advance to the next round, frogs had three jumps to reach the 15-foot mark designated by what looked like a three-point line.

At the competition entry counter, I dished out three bucks to rent a frog. Then I marked the box on the entry form that read, "Yes, I will jockey my own frog." Damn right I would jockey my own frog. I'm a National League fan. I don't approve of the designated hitter and I don't hold with substitute frog jockeys. "Where do I get my saddle?" I asked the lady at the counter. She didn't laugh much at that one. I think she had heard it before.

As I stepped up to the stage, I gazed at the men running the show and realized that this was serious business. They were dressed in full cowboy regalia: 10-gallon hats, spurs and pistols slung at the hips. They didn't smile much and treated the whole affair as if they were rounding up rattlesnakes.

Why are they armed? I thought to myself. Maybe it had something to do with security. Maybe to keep the frogs from stampeding.

The master of ceremonies called my name and the frog's over the microphone. Mark Twain, whose short story made this whole affair possible, featured a frog named Daniel. I named mine Fat Somers, after an old friend who had chosen to through-hike the Appalachian Trail as an odd weight-loss program. Somers wasn't much of a leaper or track star, but the guy had spunk. A man reached into a burlap bag and hoisted out a gangly looking creature. "I gotcha a goodun'," he said. "He's a jumper all right!"

I had studied the technique of a young girl who competed right before me. She sprayed the frog with a light mist of water, stretched the fellow vertically, wrung him out and plopped him on the starting mark. Then she dropped to her knees behind him and hollered, "JUMP!" Out of either fear, shock or desperation, that frog leaped a total of 16 feet. Not bad, but a hair shy of the world record of 21 feet, 5 3/4 inches, set by Rosie the Ribbiter in 1986.

I stretched out my frog, who measured about a foot, and plopped him down on the starting "lily." Slapping the ground behind him, I let out the customary "JUMP!" Fat Somers didn't budge. Maybe I hadn't chosen the right name. I gave another holler. Three jumps later we racked up a grand total of 6 feet, 4 inches. So what if we were out after the first round and outclassed by an 11-year-old. I was a certified frog jockey and proud of it.

With all of the foolishness behind me, I returned my attention to a more serious pursuit—science. Sure, the chips were down. The place didn't seem wild enough for animal experimentation. The jumping competition was placid. But, I should have expected that. Your frog dunkers probably didn't conduct business in such well-lit areas, where the law might slap the cuffs on. But my hopes brightened on the way to the margarita stand.

A certain wildness hung in the air. A crowd of big buckle-wearin', hat wavin' cow folk whistled at some kind of ranch animal roundup in the Promenade of Horses Display Area. At the county fair, screaming children flocked around the haunted house, and Ozzy Osbourne's greatest hits blared from the speakers at the Rockin' Roller Coaster Ride. Anarchy hadn't broken out yet, but I could easily imagine the whole lot degenerating into a frog dunking frenzy. Finally, I came to the margarita stand sitting right next to the cowboy poetry tent. Cowboys...liquor. Sometimes positioning is everything. My spirits soared.

I expected to find a frenzied crowd huddled behind the liquor tent yelling, "Dunk him again. He ain't dead yet!" To my disappointment, I found happy hour. A beer-bellied man in black T-shirt (emblazoned with an American eagle) stood cocked on one leg, sipping a margarita and chatting politely with someone who looked a lot like my grandmother. No frog baptism. No experiments to test one of science's greatest claims. Here was the largest gathering of frogs in the world—tequila on hand—and not one ruffian testing the theory.

You'd think that with bikers, cowboys and wild children on hand the frogs wouldn't stand a chance.

That's it. I'd had enough. It was all up to me. I would grab a drink and apprehend the nearest frog. So I bellied up to the window, flashed my Nevada driver's license...and got flat denied. "We can't accept an out of state I.D.," said the concessionaire.

"What? How can this be the *International* Frog Jumping Contest if you can't even take out of state I.D.?"

"Sorry," replied the man behind the window. "Boss' orders."

At that moment, my experiment died, and science will probably suffer for it. Take all that crap you've heard about the "wild" nature of Californians and trash it. The bikers were polite, the cowboys hadn't fired a shot and the general fairgoers behaved like church folk at a Sunday social. I should have lived during the '60s, when people weren't afraid to experiment.

Now I'm back home where my I.D. can get me a drink at any bar, but my frog can't make it past the front door. While I now know that frogs and "hogs" get along just fine, I may never prove that frogs can't survive in margaritas. But I'm going back next year. The same article on page 14 claims, "Some frogs can be frozen and survive." This I've got to see.

Murphy Rules

By Rick Sanger

"Man-O-Manischwitz! This water is butt-cold!" I often start talking to myself after four or five days alone in the backcountry. But this ethnic theme was a new twist. Maybe the icy slush nibbling at my shins was somehow causing my Jewish genes to express themselves. I am Jewish. Or rather, Jew-ish, like some birds are brown-ish: sort of brown, but not so much so that you'd expect to see either of us in temple on Friday nights.

"Jesus Christ!"

Philosophizing no more, I spun around in the freezing water and quickly made for dry ground, gingerly stepping over the pea-sized gravel that now felt like upturned tacks. I sat down on a warm chunk of granite and picked up my right foot. Rubbing hurt more than it helped, so I just held it and made chimpanzee noises to hasten the rewarming (ouu! ouu! eee! ah! ah! ah!).

It was my first week as a backcountry ranger in the Sierra; a dream job finally come true. For three years I had prepared and politicked. I'd taken courses that ranged from first aid to federal law, from shooting shotguns to shooting rapids. I'd learned how to surreptitiously search suspicious structures for stealthful scumbags; and to heartily hunt hellish heights for hikers in hazard. And now, at last, I was doing the real work: strolling about by myself through beautiful and benign wilderness, exploring thousands of acres of sugar pine and lodgepole forests, gazing devoutly at towering granite domes that shone white in the sun. "Maybe," I thought, "I've finally found a job right for me."

Don't get me wrong. I would have certainly been willing to risk life and limb for the safety of the park visitor, but there were no visitors! It had been a big winter, and the snow still on the trails had deterred people from the day's trck to my patrol area. So I had to enjoy it all myself.

I was now at a spot where two lakes touched, a narrow point where a bridge made from a single log allowed hikers to pass without having to wade the waist-deep water, or alternatively, wander several rocky miles around the lake's periphery. Or rather, there used to be a log bridge here. Now it was a 30-foot-wide, icy passage. A veritable Bering Strait—similar species were destined to evolutionarily diverge on either side rather than brave the chilly crossing. Warming temperatures had increased the runoff, and the lake water was accordingly high. The log that used to span the distance had floated away a few days earlier as I had stepped from it when returning from my first patrol of the area. Since most of the lake was still frozen, it only floated 100 feet or so before the current had lodged it against the slush and ice that covered the rest of the lake. Only at this narrow point, where one lake drained into the next, was the water surface thawed. The log was mockingly close, but uselessly distant.

Maybe it was through perception distorted by solitude that I took this situation personally. This was not a simple case of chance; it was my weight that had dislodged the log, so it was my fault the bridge was gone. The way I saw it, my first act on the job had been to destroy a key bridge on what would be a major thoroughfare once the snow melted. Not good. So now I was back to rebuild the bridge, envisioning that my report would tell only the important part of the story: "Repaired log bridge allowing passage of Pacific Crest Trail hikers." That would look good. It had to look good—my rehire status depended on it.

I looked out over the lake toward the ex-bridge, the log, the problem at hand. "Reach, throw, go," is what they say in lifesaving courses. Reaching wasn't an option, so I had tried throwing a rock with a nylon cord tied onto it, thinking it might somehow hook over the log and allow me to pull it back to shore. Instead, the rock had fallen short and punched through the slush. It was now irretrievable; pulling on the cord raised the rock into the underside of the ice floe where it wedged itself more firmly into place with every tug. The cord now lay clearly visible on the surface of the frozen lake, and wound its way from where the ice anchor was imbedded, back to where I was sitting. Its sinuous trail casually told the whole story of my ineptitude. My attempt to pull from a slightly different angle by wading a few feet into the lake had evoked some musing about my Jewish roots, but left the cord, the rock and the log firmly in place.

The sun and the glittering blue water were hypnotic. The current passing through the narrows made a soothing, bubbling noise, and the trees on the foreign shore stood tall and proud in their new isolation. By now, feeling had returned to my feet, and the sun warmed my ankles and calves deliciously, and made my green uniform pants almost hot to the touch. It would be bad if Jim saw me idle like this. He was my supervisor and a borderline fanatic. That is, he actually supervised. He had told me that he monitors new rangers closely, and I knew that he had a nasty habit of hiking the trails unannounced to check up on things. It seemed somehow unfair. I mean, I was working for the federal government now, wasn't I entitled to some sort of free ride?

Reach, throw, go.

Suddenly, it was clear to me. This was a time for action. Sunning myself on the shore, waiting for the log to come magically floating over to me would not make a good entry in my monthly activity report. But the word "initiative" was popular back at headquarters, a nice sounding word, the kind of word that could help my career.

A raft is what I needed, and the design of it filled my mind as I strode back to my cabin, which was only a quarter mile back down the trail. Did I have enough wood to float it? No. But I did have a pile of old Therm-A-Rest pads. What could I use as a deck? I walked right past volcanoes that puckered forth colored balloons behind grizzly bear and bighorn sheep singing duets arm-in-arm in fields of roses. Or could have, anyway, but I would have seen none of it. Nor would I have cared. Only the raft mattered now. The raft, the log, my job. I gathered the supplies I needed, returned to the lake's shore, and went about constructing my vehicle of genius.

The raft took shape just as I had planned it. I folded four Therm-A-Rest pads in half and wrapped them with duct tape to keep them from springing back open. The now double-thick pads were for floatation. On top of them, I placed a piece of plywood that was just big enough for me to kneel on. Using nylon cord, I bound the pads to the underside of the plywood and tightened the whole thing together with a trucker's hitch. Duct tape, trucker's hitch and a sunny day. Wilderness life was good.

I was pumped. Proudly, I carried the craft to the lake's edge and slid it into the slushy water. It felt firm when I leaned on it, so I gingerly climbed aboard. It was stable, remarkably stable. I pushed through the slush using a camp shovel as a paddle. The job was as good as done. I dreamed briefly about the days ahead that I would spend fishing from this fine craft. I considered how an outrigger extension would allow me to lie down and take afternoon naps while drifting across the glittering water, that is, once the lake completely thawed.

A sudden lurch to starboard interrupted my reverie. The imbalance felt like a passenger had just jumped off one side. I turned around sharply, and realized that it had been the slush-laden water bordering the lake shore that had made the craft so stable. Now I was clear from that layer and truly "in deep water." My arms flailed to correct the imbalance, but too much so. The Titanic lurched to port. I lurched to starboard. But my shovel caught the tail of the trucker's hitch, which, out of habit, I had tied with a quick-release bow. The tension in the nylon-cord popped loose. I yelped the universal cry for holy intervention (the "S" word), as the first of the Therm-A-Rest pads shot out from under the plywood to the east. I promised to live a holy life (the "F" word), as the second Therm-A-Rest shot toward the west. Just for a moment, I sank straight down, like the unreal pause in a cartoon catastrophe, then the plywood pivoted sharply and pitched me into the icy depths. I grabbed one of the pads floating nearby and clung to it for dear life.

Warning: The instructions specifically advise against using Therm-A-Rest pads as floatation devices. So what was I thinking? I'll tell you: Cold! Cold! Cold! Cold!

I thrashed and kicked, desperately trying to swim to shore. My boots felt like some high-tech device designed to slip through the water without resistance, save for the slightest sinking pull. My pile jacket was an icy weight. I tried to swim faster in the numbing water, but I couldn't feel if my limbs were moving at all. I struggled hard in a losing battle to keep my gasping mouth above the frothing water. My body was distant, an anchor at the end of my neck. An icy wave went down my throat; I coughed, choked and spat. I was going down.

Luckily, and unbeknownst to me, my arms and legs were still moving after all. I realized this when one foot kicked a rock on the bottom, hard. The thump, though deadened, trumpeted salvation. I kicked the bottom again. Yes! I got a little closer, gained some purchase, then lunged toward shore. Immediately I buckled from the weight of my clothes and the weakness of my legs, and lay only half out of the water for some time. But red lights were flashing in my brain. I knew I had to pull my clothes off or die of hypothermia. My fingers were as useful as corndogs. Zippers were almost impossible and boot lace knots were out of the question; I cut them with my survival knife. Once stripped, I lay down on my stomach on a flat, warm rock while feeling slowly began to return: the feeling of a thousand nails jabbing into my body. But this only lasted a few lifetimes, and eventually left me only extremely cold. I gathered the strength to roll onto my back just in time to see a cloud pass in front of the sun. Next to that cloud was a slightly bigger, darker cloud. The effective temperature dropped 20 degrees, and a puff of wind blew by from the north. I closed my eyes and tried to ignore the cold. I willed the clouds to disperse and the sun to climb back to its noon position. I visualized hot sand beneath me, the sound of rolling surf in the distance and a bucket brigade of waiters to bring me hot chocolate. A frigid gust sent the waiters running for shelter. God, I hate reality. No exclamation would have helped, ethnic or not. Only a moan surfaced as I climbed to my feet, grabbed my hat (the only dry clothing nearby) and hobbled to the leeward side of a large boulder. The rock was still warm from the sun, and I pressed my body against the side of it to soak in as much of the warmth as I could.

Arms outstretched hugging a huge boulder, wearing nothing but goose bumps and a ranger's hat, I heard the idle chatter of hikers come to my ears. My eyes shot open. Sure enough, I was only a foot off the trail. I hopped back toward my soggy clothes, but not before the hikers rounded the corner and saw my better side slipping off into the bushes. The tone of their conversation took a turn, and I listened from behind another rock.

"God, do you think it's safe? I don't want some creep jumping out of the bushes at me."

"I think it'll be OK, Honey. But we can go back to the ranger station we passed to report it, if you want."

"Not likely," I thought, and moved to a spot where I could watch the couple disappear back down the trail toward my cabin. I was about to get up when I heard another hiker approaching from the other direction. "Why is everyone showing up now?" I asked myself. "Must be Murphy's Law." But it wasn't Murphy I saw on the trail. Murphy doesn't wear a Sam Brown belt, a gray uniform shirt, and the badge of a National Park Service Ranger next to a name plate that says "Jim—Backcountry Supervisor."

I ducked down fast and nearly fell over. His footsteps hesitated, then passed on. I backed away from my hiding place. My clothes were still too soggy to be of any use, so I just slipped on my boots and left the pile there. "This can't be happening. This just can't be happening..." Murmuring this over and over, my new mantra, I made my way, off-trail, toward my cabin.

The cabin is situated on a spur trail about 200 yards long that leaves the main trail toward the south. I was on the south side, too, and by choosing my route carefully, I was able to approach the cabin quietly from the back side. I put my back side down on a nearby boulder and listened, trying to locate all the players. One, two, three voices! Jim was talking with the other two hikers about halfway down the spur trail, leaving it relatively safe for me to sneak in through the back door of the cabin. This I did, and quickly put on my warmest long underwear (feels so good!) and a clean uniform, all without being detected. Relieved, I stepped out onto the balcony with an air to see what all the commotion was about. The word "hat" drifted to me through the trees. I took mine off, tossed it back through the cabin door, and sauntered down the trail toward the group.

Jim greeted me and filled me in on the situation. Apparently, we had a possible 51-50 (ranger code for crazy person) harassing visitors on the trail. I nodded, reached for the notebook in my uniform pocket, and poised myself professionally with pen in hand. Jim continued, "White male, approximately 5 feet 11 inches, naked except for a green hat." I shifted my weight a bit as I wrote, hoping to look shorter.

"No unique identifying marks. He was seen out by the log bridge."

I winced.

The visitors thanked us and, deciding they had had enough for one day, turned around and headed back toward the trailhead.

"Let's check it out," Jim said, and started walking to the scene of the crime.

"Right," I replied, and fell in pace behind him. "Think this was just some guy sunbathing?" I suggested.

"Sounds like some weirdo to me. Who would sunbathe in the middle of the trail? And what kind of tan could you expect to get in this weather?" He was right. The wind was now steady and cold. My suggestion had floated about as well as my raft had.

I couldn't stop thinking about the pile of wet clothes up ahead, which included a very wet uniform shirt with my name plate pinned to it. I agonized over whether I should confess the whole thing now. I felt cheap hiding the truth, trying to think of some scheme to protect my interests. I looked down at my badge and uniform; those symbols of public trust hung heavy on my shoulders. I knew what I had to do, what being a law-enforcement officer demanded that I do.

"Why don't I look on the south side of the trail for this deviant," I suggested, "while you check the north side for tracks?" He bought it.

In the few minutes I had alone, I carefully hid my clothes and the raft parts in a nearby bush. The pine needles and undergrowth absorbed the trail of drips that would have given me away.

The scene looked pretty clean by the time Jim showed up. "Found a couple of tracks on the trail," he said, "Someone wasn't wearing shoes. Looked like they came this way. What'd you find?"

"Well..." I began, but he cut me off.

"Oh, yeah. Fair bit of disturbance in this area." His eyes followed some track I couldn't see, until he was staring out at a nylon cord lying out on the ice. "What the...?" He walked over to the cord and tugged on it a few times. The end held fast. He pulled harder and the rope stiffened. He grabbed it with both hands, leaned back hard with his full weight and heaved into it. Without warning the stone popped free of the slush and came rocketing toward us. I dove for the ground where he was already sprawled as it shot past. A loud "pop" echoed over the lake when the rock ricocheted off a tree. It landed in some nearby bushes...some very familiar looking bushes! No shit! Jim got up and started coiling the rope, theorizing about how the cord came to be where he had found it. He walked toward the end of the rope, toward the bushes, toward my clothes, toward the end of my short career. But he was pulling in the cord at the same time. Was he reeling in the rock, or was Murphy reeling him in? It was going to be close. I sat down; my legs would no longer hold me. I saw the rock come bouncing out of the undergrowth toward him. Dragging behind it, by a single thread, was one, brown, standard-issue sock. My head dropped into my hands.

"You OK?" Jim asked, "Look kinda sick."

"No," I said, and looked up. The sock was lying 5 feet from him, but the cord was fully coiled in his hands.

"No," I said again. "I must still be adjusting to the drinking water. Would you mind if we went back to the cabin? I can fill you in on things there."

"No need to report, Rick, I've seen enough. Got to be moving along anyway. Tell me if you hear anything more of this pervert. Meantime, get that log bridge back into place. Damn nuisance to ford the lake. Use that log there. Looks like it should work fine."

"Yeah, but..." I looked over toward the log. To hell with it. I couldn't take it any longer. I was ready to admit failure. If he wanted to use that log for the bridge, he could damn-well go swimming out there and get the thing himself. But the log wasn't there!

"Problem?" he asked.

Then I spotted the log he was pointing at, my log, now bobbing gently against the shore, very near where I had done my human icicle act. The steady winds had dislodged it from the ice and pushed it to where it was now giggling.

"No problem," I finally answered.

"Good. Then I'll see you next week." He walked back toward the trail. Before disappearing from sight he turned and shouted over his shoulder, "And when you're done, don't leave any of your stuff lying around in the bushes!"

I sat where I was for a long time, alternately shaking my head in disbelief, making rude gestures at the log, and laughing out loud.

"Oy vey, such a day!"

Human Pocket Lint

By Michael Hodgson

Countless times I have turned my pockets inside out to empty lint that had somehow gathered since the last laundering, pausing to watch it scatter before the wind. I never once thought that I would have occasion to relate to those bits of fluff and dirt, yet there I was, blowing ass over teakettle like so much pocket lint of the mountain gods, dumped unceremoniously onto the snowfields of Mount Washington to be whisked away by 100 mile per hour winds.

I have long known that Mount Washington, New Hampshire, has a reputation of being a somewhat ornery hostess to those who choose to wander around her broad flanks and summit. She's sometimes congenial, sometimes full of venom and those who risk traveling unprepared into her world risk a backpack full of hurt, even death. Mount Washington is such a temperamental mistress that the self-proclaimed caretakers, the Appalachian Mountain Club, have posted neatly carved wooden signs at various trailheads advising against proceeding beyond those signs unless properly dressed and carrying emergency clothing, food and the like. At the bottom of each sign is a gentle reminder that many have died on the mountain, even in summer.

Perhaps I was tempting fate, choosing to climb to the summit in late November to observe a nationally known tent company test its winter tents—the ultimate evaluation of quality in my opinion. True enough, I would be staying with permission in the protected embrace of the Mount Washington Observatory building once on the summit, but I would still have to get myself up there and back down in one piece—no easy feat if the mountain, which has the world's worst recorded weather conditions on earth, decided to go ballistic with me clinging to her flanks.

The hike up the mountaineer's route out of Tuckerman's Ravine was uneventful. A bright, warming sun shone down on Hal and me as we worked our way up over ice-clad boulders to the summit and the Mount Washington Observatory. Distant clouds looked somewhat ominous, but the sun and beauty of the moment chased away any lingering doubts. What a place, what a mountain! Gordon, Gretchen, Steve, Fred, Dan and my climbing partner, Hal, were a little perturbed, however. The winds were only gusting to 45 mph—not exactly the kind of conditions desirable for a quality four-season tent evaluation.

A storm's arrival blew away their concern the following morning, bringing winds gusting to 75 mph and driving pellets of snow before it. We played all day, setting up tents, attaching electrodes to the poles, and watching Dan record the various stresses placed on the aluminum poles. Visibility deteriorated to about 10 feet by evening.

That night, the winds picked up with a vengeance, gusting to 120 mph. Feeling a little nutty, we all ventured up onto the roof of the observatory. I tried doing jumping jacks—seemed like a good idea at the time—and found that whenever I jumped, the wind would hurl me backward landing me on my feet about two yards from my point of takeoff...WILD! Visibility at this point was almost zero. We were supposed to leave the next day, but if the weather kept up like this, departure would be impossible.

Morning dawned overcast and just as surly. The winds were gusting to 115 mph although visibility had increased to a whopping 5 feet. All we could do was watch the gauges and wait. Since any window that might open up was likely to be a narrow one, we waited packed and ready to go at a moment's notice. Minutes ticked by slowly as it approached noon. Another storm was on the heels of this one, so if we didn't get respite from the pounding weather, our stay was likely to be a very long one indeed.

Just as tedium was merging with monotony, the window we were praying for opened. According to the weather gurus in the observatory, the weather had lifted enough to let us make a run for it. In this case, lifted meant steady wind at 90 mph with gusts upward of 100 mph and an accompanying windchill of minus 150 degrees Fahrenheit. Lifted, my ass, but there was no more time to wait. We tied in to the length of rope I had prepared, slung ice axes from our wrists, cinched down parka hoods, pulled on our goggles and braced ourselves for battle. We elected to leave our crampons strapped to our packs instead of our feet since the blowing snow was drifting so deeply that they would probably become more of a hindrance than a help. Of course, we also realized that there would be those few times when the snow might be blown completely off the mountain's shoulder, leaving us skittering and scratching on a surface of ice that would be as slippery as a greased pig.

The door swung open and we launched ourselves into a surreal world of translucent light and an unceasing, howling wind that would snatch spoken words and hurl them away to tumble unheard amid the swirling flakes of snow. Visibility was about 20 feet, so it was just possible to make out the first couple of shadowy figures on the rope ahead of me. Snow pellets, driven by the 100-mph gusts of wind, hissed over my boots and across the surface of my parka.

Each tentative step was like walking across the backs of a herd of bucking broncs, all surging and heaving. I'd step, encounter a massive gust of wind, lurch, stagger, catch my balance, lean into the wind to counter the gust and then nearly fall over again when the gust subsided to a mere 90 mph.

My breath quickly condensed and then froze on the outside of my balaclava, sealing me in behind a thin coating of ice making breathing difficult and adding to an impending feeling of claustrophobia. Claustrophobia?! That was rich. Here I was, standing in the middle of the great outdoors, as far away from a closed in feeling as I could get, but still feeling claustrophobic because swaddled in layers of clothing that were slowly becoming encased in ice, I feared mummification.

Ripping off a mitten, I clawed at my face and tugged the balaclava away from my mouth. As I gasped at the air, icy needles blasted my face and the cold that roared in on me threatened to suck the breath out of my lungs. In seconds, my skin went numb. One of my lips cracked and began to bleed, until the blood froze. It was so cold, I was only vaguely aware of the metallic taste of blood on my tongue. This was weird.

To make matters worse, my new goggles, ones I was testing for another company, began to freeze up. Five minutes into our escape from the summit, with me supposedly bringing up the rear as the solid anchor of our team, and my visibility was reduced to nil. I could hardly make out the silhouette of Gretchen in front of me, and so I struggled to time my pace based on the amount of sag I could make out in the rope between us. Several times, the rope snapped taut, tugging on her, stopping her forward momentum causing her to jerk the rope of the person in front of her—a mountaineer's domino game.

"Jesus! Sorry...sorry," I would mumble to no one in particular.

Repeatedly I pulled my goggles away from my eyes and down over my mouth, breathing heavily into them for a few seconds to melt the ice before I snapped them back onto my face. My efforts served little purpose, however, because while the goggles were off, the cold and wind were so intense that the tears which formed around my eyes as a result of the stinging onslaught froze and as soon as I put my goggles back on, they froze again, too. I had a vague sense that the mountain was enjoying this.

One-half mile and one-half hour into our trek to drop down off the summit and out of the wind, we entered the danger zone—a few hundred yards of windswept ridgeline with a hard-packed and slippery surface that had been scrubbed smooth and clean by the wind. Leaning heavily into the wind, angled at a ridiculous 30 degrees, our team stomped forward. There was a rhythm to the madness: jam the ice axe into the ice ahead, lean on it and then kick, kick with each foot, finding security and foothold in the tiniest indent scuffed into the surface. Several times, the wind drove me to my knees and threatened to sweep me off the mountain altogether.

We inched across the exposed ridge taking what seemed like an eternity to move only 100 yards. Suddenly, the mountain appeared to mistake Gretchen for a fallen leaf and tossed her before a mighty gust of wind. It was somewhat comical to see a human being lifted off of the ground, whirled and tumbled before falling to earth in a jumbled pile of fabric and rope that was subsequently blown across the ridge like so much dust. Humorous that is until the force of her fall coupled with the wind's sudden increase in intensity ripped both Steve, just ahead of Gretchen on the rope, and me off of our feet, too, and sent us tumbling across the hard-packed snow.

Crampons would have been a good idea, but they're kind of hard to put on with frozen fingers in the teeth of a gale that threatened to blow me into another time zone. As it was, it felt rather foolish fighting for traction with a perfectly good pair of crampons attached to the back of my pack. Shoulda, coulda, woulda, but didn't—a fool's epitaph on a lonely gravestone.

The sensation was rather strange, I must admit. I was powerless for a moment against the wind's strength, as my 160 pounds tumbled and skittered across the hard-packed snow like a bit of pocket lint. Somehow, the corner of my mind that was still working and not overloaded with morbid fascination convinced my body to surge into action. I whirled and sank the pick end of my ice axe into the snow, arresting my slide and Gretchen's tumble. A sideways glance up the rope revealed the entire team was now prostrate and clinging to anchored ice axes.

The good part about the slide was we ended up along a drift of snow that offered a far better foothold than we had had before. As we struggled to rise while the wind continued to unleash venom and fury on us, I was relieved to discover that this softer snow offered fairly solid traction underfoot.

One hundred more yards to go and we could drop off the ridge and put the wind behind us—those were some of the longest yards of my life. Goggles frozen, I was effectively hiking blind. The wind did its level best to pound the team into submission, but we never wavered. Sink the ice axe, lean into the wind, kick, kick, sink the ice axe, lean into the wind, kick, kick...200 baby steps to relative tranquillity. As we dropped off the ridgeline, the wind subsided to a mere 80 mph. No longer battling just to stay upright and on course, we began to double-time it off the mountain. We had made it.

As we trudged out onto the meadow leading to the trailhead and our cars, my lip began to burn. I reached up and brushed away a drop of blood. Well, at least my face was beginning to thaw. From freezing to overheating, I peeled down to my long underwear.

"Wonderful day, isn't it?" a cross-country skier shouted as he glided past.

I stood there, jacket in hand, steam streaming skyward from my damp underclothing, blood oozing from my lip, and gazed around at a calm winter scene bathed in alpenglow. Then, I glanced skyward, toward the distant summit, still shrouded in clouds where just hours ago I had clung to my sanity and the mountain's shoulder amid a tumultuous assault of wind and cold.

"Mmmm...a good day indeed, unless you amount to nothing more than pocket lint of the mountain gods," I mused.

Sanders, '96

Moscow Mantra

By Mike Ferrell

"Walking the wire is living...the rest is just waiting."
—Kari Wallenda

One fall season, my friend, who was back from summer employment, told me he had discovered a new "high." In 1969, this was considered a legitimate and, at the time, noble pursuit. I watched curiously as he squatted down next to his bed and commenced to count hyperventilations. A dozen or so deep breaths later, I watched incredulously as he held the last breath, stood up, stuck his thumb in his mouth, and blew for all he was worth as if his thumb was a plugged trumpet. His face turned crimson, his eyes bulged until he wilted onto the bed backward. Aghast, I watched as his eyes rolled up, he convulsed, then started snoring grotesquely. While I considered ambulances and explanations, he woke up ashen, wondered where he was and what had happened, whereupon I informed him if he ever did that again, I'd kill him.

For years, I had similar feelings about rock climbers: gravity's stuntmen, nomads of expanded foolishness, slaves of their own adrenaline deficiencies. Or, just plain young and stupid. Yet, in my 40s, I tried it and I liked it.

Soon I was buying climbing shoes, harness and belay device, then rope and carabiners, and eventually hexes, stoppers and cleverly engineered spring-loaded camming devices. While I measured myself on 5.7's, 5.8's and 5.9's, I dreamed of the Nose and Half Dome. I saw Royal Robbins speak and felt the presence of an elder, of a Virgil quoting Holy Man. I read *The Freedom of the Hills*, books by John Long and Daniel Duane, and befriended climbers who had actually climbed the Nose. I convinced myself while riding the recliner, beer in hand, remote at the ready, that El Cap was possible even for me. I started leading low-grade, short, single-pitch climbs. I became a part of the geometry of the sport's growth, taking many first-timers to the rock.

"I need the abyss under me. It helps me concentrate."
—Patrick Vallencant

And so it was with this momentum, I found myself one gray, windy, October morning at Smith Rock anxious to lead a multi-pitch climb called Moscow. In the Central Oregon desert, Smith Rock rises from a canyon 800 feet to its summit like a huge, colorful, castle. The aptly named Crooked River surrounds it like a moat. Counting the fourth class scramble to the top, Moscow is a 300-foot route of four pitches rated 5.6. It starts high above the Crooked River at the top of a steep slope leading from moat to castle wall. Now to real rock jocks, the priests and priestesses of the vertical gods, a 5.6 climb isn't even a walk to church, much less a pilgrimage or communion. To a lay person like myself, well, anyway you look at it, 5.6 ascends up above the earth in unusual ways. But for a future Yosemite Big Waller, this should be cake, I thought to myself.

The first pitch meandered vertical up a blocky crack system for about 100 feet. It took pro well and offered little resistance to my notions of my climbing abilities and this particular climb. There are no established belay stations on this route, as we discovered at the first belay ledge...no bolts, no chains, no webbing. So I slung webbing around a horn, placed pro here and there, and with the satisfaction that comes from that kind of self-reliance, belayed my partner up. Once John was on our little perch—the Crooked River a long ways down, mule deer wading near the far shore, browsing the grassy bank—we reorganized ourselves for the next lead, which again was mine.

Initially, a minor bulge must be surmounted, then the route follows a dihedral crack for another 150 feet. I climbed over the bulge with the right mix of anxiousness and confidence. Things were going well. My focus was the one square yard in front of my face. The cams, hexes and stoppers fit the crack just as they're designed to do, and I wasn't too frightened.

Then, gradually but steadily, my focus, my square yard, stretched inauspiciously downward to the ground. The fabric of my bluster began to unravel, the straw of my house loosened in the wind, my lion turned cowardly. "I do believe in chocks, I do believe in chocks. I do, I do, I do!"

"Cluck cluck, cluck cluck."—Mike Ferrell

Somehow I missed the second belay station. About 175 feet up, I started the self-debasement. "Who in the hell do you think you are! El Capitan, my ass! What are you doing up here?!?!" As I made dicey move after dicey move, I looked over my shoulder: the Crooked River was now a thin ribbon of glinting water; the mule deer, a blond ant. I started thinking of my TV as the Holy Grail; the couch, the shrine of my contentment. I wanted down off this rock, down to safety and linoleum floors, carpeted rooms, spring-loaded easy chairs, places where you can't fall far. The self-denigration changed tense. "Who did you think you were?!" Having given up all hope of pulling it back together, of changing fear back to spirit.

And then it happened. One of those things you want never to happen. Less than 30 feet from the top, the crack became an off width and I ran out of suitable gear to protect myself. Though where I stood was fine, no big strain, I could not picture a way up. Like many off widths, the crack offered no jagged edge to grab, nothing deep within it had features to hold, no toeholds existed on either side to step on. I could not stem or grip or jam anything, and worse, I couldn't protect any brazen move I might venture. Though the simple monosyllable word seems hugely inadequate, I was stuck—which rhymed with the word now present on my lips like a mantra. For the next 30 minutes, I clung there changing from one grip to another pondering the simplicity of life: I couldn't go up and I couldn't go down.

John's voice, meanwhile, would waft up to me on the getting colder wind from somewhere out of sight below. The words were unintelligible but the question was obvious and becoming persistent. "I'm stuck," I calmly noted in reply. More questions, perhaps in French this time. "I'm stuck," I said a little louder. Another question...in Spanish? "Yo soy stuck!" I yelled. "Istichneinorish?" he yelled, in German I think. I'd had it with this annoyance and so I screamed, "I'm fucking stuck, goddammit!"

There, it was over. I'd admitted it to the Crooked River universe and now it was time to unstick my sorry butt. As I rested there, my rack chiming in the wind, I considered down. Looking between my ankles and seeing the hundred feet of rope that dangled there disappear into the abyss, downclimbing looked tough. Even worse, it represented failure. It meant I couldn't even entertain my half-baked fantasies of Half Dome climbing glory from the Laz-E-Boy. Defeat was down. I considered remaining where I was, but I dreaded John and his multi-lingual torment and feared death by slow embarrassment. I knew when they eventually hauled my carcass off, my face would still be flush from the humiliation that was my last dying thought. "We pulled a real winner off Moscow," I could hear the rescuers sarcastically say. "Had to crowbar his hands loose." I could picture the coroner noting the cause of death: "los cajones pequenos," the word "whimp" on my toe tag at the morgue. The mortician would place me in a coffin with my hands grasping my throat as the final symbol of my life. My headstone would read: Just plain old stupid.

So I looked around. Were there other ways out? None at my skill level. From my perspective, the faces were smooth, unclimbable. Another nearby crack seemed even more difficult. Looking higher, I saw a flake about halfway between me and the belay point above. It offered decent handholds all the way to the top, if I could only get to it. Then like some small but significant miracle, I found deep in my rack a large spring-loaded cam that I was certain I'd already used. I reached up as high as I could, squeezed the trigger, slid it into the rock and clipped the rope to it. It was barely big enough for the fissure.

By now John's inquisition was moving into Eastern European languages. Compelled by this, and suddenly deep in conversation with the god of my agnosticism—"OK, God, forget those doubts, just you and me, baby!"—I started to move up. To this day, probably as a blessing from Agnogod, I remember nothing of the climb until I grabbed that flake. From there, I pulled easily to the top.

"Gravity always wins. Accept that."—Erma Bombeck

As I belayed John up, he came to my Waterloo spot, started laughing, and asked me, "What's this?" In his hand, dangling from the rope, was my big cam, a nice but worthless decoration. "Well," I said, "It was all psychological protection." He got to the top, I told him my story, and in English he offered me this: "Nice lead."

If he asks me to do it again, I'll kill him.

The Real McCoy

By John Long

If a judge ever heard this story, I might find myself in court to answer for not saying anything until now. But an inquest assumes that someone would go to the trouble of making an issue out of nothing—at least nothing they could prove. So I'll run that risk and not change any names because people should know about the great Ronnie Hart.

This all happened over a dozen years ago, my last year on the National Whitewater Kayak Team. The Olympic Job Placement Program had landed me a fake job with Finn Properties, a building and land management outfit in Los Angeles. I worked half days, and aside from changing coffee filters and photocopying documents, my duties were "honorary," as the receptionist used to say. Anyway, that summer I'd made a run down the Bio-Bio river in Chile, and one morning while I was going through some photos of it, Hank came over to my little cubical. Aside from casual hellos at the Xerox machine or in the elevator, we'd never said a word to each other. Hank picked up one of the photos, took a glance and dropped it back. "I'd heard something about you doing a little paddling."

"A little." I chuckled. I might not have known much about Hank and the other two-dozen people at Finn, but they knew about me—as a national champion and a slacker.

Hank examined another photo, this one of me cresting a 10-foot wave. "Lined up a little broach-angle here." He sounded as indifferent as if he were noting a typo on a deed. "Probably flipped right after this picture was taken."

In fact, I had flipped. For a moment, I sat there wondering how a property manager could glance at the photo and know what followed.

"You must be pretty handy on the water to spot my mistake here."

"You run the big water, you make mistakes," Hank said, and picked the photo back up. "But it's been some time since I made one this silly."

I froze. I'd been the North American whitewater champion for three years running. My entire life was tied to paddling. Hank might as well have kicked me in the balls and told me I deserved worse.

"We'll have to team up some time," I said, "so you can show me how it's done."

Hank reached down and scribbled his address onto a legal pad full of doodles and boat designs. "Swing on by the house tonight and maybe we can talk about it. If you want."

"Count on it."

I felt like jumping up on my desk and yelling, "Can you believe the cheek of this guy?" But the only thing around me were filing cabinets; and the people down the hall in the cramped offices had families and mortgages and long hours at Finn and were about as interested in my paddling as I was on lease contracts and delinquent renters.

It might have been that I'd suffered Hank's handling by myself—and had to like it—then maybe it was the flip way he'd pointed up my mistake in the photo, perhaps still the certainty with which he assured me he wouldn't have done the same. Whatever it was, rolling toward Hank's house that night, I never was so keen to drag a person onto a fiendish river and see him swallow half of it.

Hank lived way out of town, and he answered the door wearing an old pair of Nike gym trunks, his body glistening with sweat and black graphite dust. He looked extremely fit, like he'd been jimmied off a Roman frieze and struck to life. But along the left side of his back, the skin was all scarred and crinkly. An old burn of some kind, and a nasty one.

"Come on in and grab a beer," he said, pulling me inside. He scanned the dark night and quickly closed the door.

His house was not much of a home, rather a warehouse of kayaks, paddles, resin, float bags and tools, every room a workshop except for the one papered in maps and photos. Hank fetched a couple beers, then showed me his boats. Most were experimental designs. A few were expertly fashioned with Kevlar and carbon fiber, but most were roto-molded plastic. Each bore a little design which I thought was American Indian—thunderbirds, and stuff like that—but I didn't ask. My eyes ran from the resin fumes. We'd hardly settled into the chart room when Hank grew so intense that I thought the fumes had gotten to him.

"Can you paddle the desperate stuff or not? And be honest, or it might cost you your life."

I'd had enough of Hank talking down to me like a weekend hacker. "Where do you get off saying that kind of crazy shit?"

"I'm talking about big, wild water," Hank said gravely, "Not slalom gates. They're very different disciplines, and I don't want to get you killed."

"You know, Hank, you've been talking in circles since you came over to my desk this morning. What's on your mind?"

Hank smiled. "I went down to try and run the Rio Juarez last weekend, but I could see right off it was too much to run alone. You join me on another shot, I'll pay for the copter and all that."

I'd never seen the Rio Juarez, but everyone who had, agreed it was suicidal. It occurred to me that Hank was mad. He looked mad, glowering there with those crazy eyes. But my pride and the challenge he'd served up wouldn't let me write him off outright.

"I'll look at it."

"It's perfectly runable, but not solo."

"Like I said, I'll take a look."

"Fine," Hank said, "but if we're paddling together, you've got to play by my rules."

I couldn't imagine what these rules would entail, but it didn't take Hank long to lay them out.

"You can never mention any of our runs to anybody. It's all a game with me, see—paddling alone, just keeping to myself. That's why I've never had you over until tonight. Now I need you."

He let that settle in, but it never really did, and wouldn't for months. Hank went into the kitchen, returned with a couple more beers and sat back in an old sofa covered with serapes.

"Maybe I'll explain it to you later," he said, handing me a beer, "but for now, if you swear to secrecy, I'll have you running rapids you never thought even remotely possible. I can't promise that you'll live long enough to take credit for them, though."

I jumped to my feet and paced around. "You got a license to make such jackass statements," I said, "or does it just come naturally to you?" So far as I knew, Hank's only credentials were a forceful personality and a knack for outlandish remarks.

"Once we get on the water, I trust you'll understand."

"I trust I will, but it's not going to be on the Juarez—not straight-a-way. And by the way, you know that everyone who's ever seen the Juarez says you'd never get off it alive."

"I've seen it, and I say otherwise," Hank came back. "Are we on, or not?"

"I've never seen you paddle a stroke, Hank. We'll do a warm-up first, and take it from there."

"Fair enough."

"How bout the Tuolumne?" That gauntlet of white water was no warm-up, except one for the next life.

"Whatever," Hank said. His urgent edge had left him in a stroke, replaced by something almost melancholy. I had the feeling that I could have suggested paddling over Victoria Falls and Hank would have said "whatever." Next day, we both called in sick and were on the water before noon.

A week of Sierra storms had drained into the river, and treacherous high water raged west into the San Joaquin Valley. As we slipped into wetsuits, I told Hank he'd better be the ace he claimed or he'd be paddling through the pearly gates in about 50 yards. He flashed me that grin of his, and cranked out into the stout current. I fell in behind. Over the first quarter mile, I saw that Hank was a superb paddler. After another quarter mile, I realized he was peerless. Then he cut loose.

He would slalom through jagged wash rocks, then bow forward, plunging the nose of his kayak into a wave. His boat would submarine in, then pop straight up and flop endwise into the eye of a boiling vortex, where he'd loop around and fire downstream— underwater. He'd crab his boat sideways through steaming rapids, logrolling, over and over. And he ran an entire stretch backward.

Whatever he did, no matter how apparently dangerous and improbable, he did it perfectly. It seemed as though the more outrageous he got, the more the river obliged him. Here I was trying to survive, while Hank clowned through rapids that had snuffed more than one expert. I had never seen anything like it. And for that matter, I'd seen and beaten every world champion in the last six years. Hank never stopped for a break or scouted ahead, lest we "cheat the creek of the little it can offer." We powered through a normal day's run in less than four hours.

On the drive home, Hank gripped the wheel and silently stared ahead. A jocund, riotous bundle of raw energy on the water, he'd crawled into a funk and had slammed the door behind him. But this mood swing astonished me less than his talent, and I kept wondering where to start and what questions to ask. After an hour on the road he hadn't said a word, hadn't even looked over at me. Finally I couldn't hack it any longer. Never mind all that paddling in secret business or his ferocious silence. Nobody could possibly get to Hank's level by paddling in a vacuum. Somebody *must* have seen him *somewhere*.

"So who did you compete for, Hank?"

"Never did."

"Well, what other great paddlers have you run with?"

"None. Besides you." That comment should have pleased me, but it vexed me even more.

"What's with the secret agent bit, Hank?"

"We had an agreement. We're going to paddle together, and that's it. That's what we agreed on, remember?" The whole thing was crazy, but I didn't press it.

"Fine, Hank. But if you just saw a guy long jump the Grand Canyon, you'd be curious. Believe me." That cut through it.

"This seems like a crackpot way to do things, I know," Hank said, for the first time glancing over at me. "But just bear with me for awhile. We'll get to it. We'll get to it all, I hope." And we headed on down the road in silence.

Though Hank otherwise stayed strictly to himself, he was dying for company and thought nothing of calling me up at two in the morning. He'd start talking about rivers we'd just run or were going to run, then we'd move on to flying saucers, reincarnation and anything else that had a facet of the marvelous in it. Hank was inquisitive in a restless, eccentric kind of way; but I came to recognize in those calls a man reaching out from a place so desolate it has no name in any language. His only salvation came on the water. That devil-may-care grin would creep over his face, and three strokes into a run he'd be paddling 10 feet off the water and screaming like a kid on a roller coaster. But by the time we'd loaded up the boats and snuck off down the road, he was already crashing back down to zero. I'd seen it time after time and could never figure it.

Four months passed before the Rio Juarez came into form, and we were plenty active in the meantime. We hit a score of furious rivers, or "rooks," as Hank called them: the Moyle, the Kayan, the Coruh in flood. For a while I wrote Hank's wizardry off to flat-out talent; only later would I understand that he whipped the impossible because he wasn't afraid if the impossible won.

He didn't ignore the consequences, rather he loathed them, and would taunt and howl at the meanest rapids. Then he'd slip into a run and, once again, the river seemed to be made just for him. The effect was contagious, and over time, I fell in behind him and started charging into fuming geysers and hydraulics, rarely opting for sane water on the flanks. The notion was to dare the consequences and trust the river. After a dozen outings, I'd picked up several of Hank's stunts, though to a far lesser degree; but I could never fathom how he ran those Class 6 rapids backward.

Once, when we were driving back from New Mexico, he started talking about the desert, then about a Navajo girl he'd known years before, and I thought he was finally going to bare himself. But he couldn't find the words, and his drift just floated out over the lone and level sand and blew away. I suppose a line of thought can supply its own seclusion. But more than Hank trying to shut the world out, he seemed always drawn into a reflection or a feeling he could never escape and that I could never be party to. Whatever, for all the months we spent together, he was often little more than a physical presence, another body at my side, stroking downriver.

The things he'd do to avoid other paddlers were incredible. He'd yank his boat off the water and into cover if he saw *anybody* on the river. Once, on the Lower Merced, we holed up in a reed thicket for more than three hours to avoid passing a camp of rafters in daylight. We ran the last six miles in scant moonlight, and completely trashed our boats on rocks we never saw. Whatever his reasons, Hank was terrified of being seen. That much I was sure of. He particularly feared coming upon commercial rafters. From that first trip down the Tuolumne, I knew Hank *had* to have competed at some time. Or some notable had at least seen or heard about him. After our moonlight debacle on the Lower Merced, the mystery grabbed my imagination and never let go. I finally called my old coach, Dan Lamay, and asked him if he'd ever heard of a paddler named Hank Crawford.

"Don't think so," he said.

"Yeah, I figured as much. Dan, I've been paddling with a guy who's about twice as good as anybody you've ever seen. Can you remember any phenoms from way back—this guy's probably in his mid-30s, at least."

"Well, there were standouts, but not like you're talking about. And anyway, you saw all those other guys: Mittan, Gerwald, Montenegro..."

Yeah, I had competed against all of those guys.

The conversation drifted to old friends and what everybody was doing, and just as I was accepting that Hank had actually sprung from the blue, Dan chimed back in.

"You know, before Edwards stopped coaching he used to talk about a kid named Hurt, or Huttle, or something like that. I think he was only with the team a short time before he got tossed in jail. I do know he raced against Accomazzo in a world-cup meet over in Italy, and beat him pretty handily."

Accomazzo was a legendary, five-time world champion. By the time I was good enough to race against him, he was almost 40, and he still beat me.

"Supposedly, he crushed him," Dan added, "but I don't know. That had to be 15 years ago, at least, and I wasn't there."

It took me two days to track down Edwards, who was living with a daughter in Boca Raton, Florida. His voice sounded breathy and labored.

"Hart. His name was Ronnie Hart," the old coach corrected. "He was only with the team long enough to compete in one international regatta, over in Corsica, and he won that one by more than 20 seconds. They thought he ran an illegal boat, or was hopped up on amphetamines, and so on. They just couldn't believe an unknown, 19-year-old kid could crush the world's best, but Hart did. And with ease. But let me tell you, as good as he was running gates, his real genius was in big white water. We'd take training runs down the Snake and Tuolumne, and the kid was pure magic. Sumbitch would run entire sections backward."

"So where is he, coach?" There was a long pause.

"Oh, he's dead now. Died fighting fires in Sequoia. He was a little wild, Hart was, and he plowed his car off the road and his girlfriend got killed. The judge found him negligent, and sentenced him hard—like five years. You know they got convicts fighting fires these days. Hart and a couple others got caught on a ridge. Ronnie Hart never made it off that ridge."

I smiled.

"So coach, did this Hart ever use any weird gear?"

"And how. He'd run these homemade jobs all painted up with Navajo designs. You know, he grew up with the Indians up by Lee's Ferry, on the Colorado River."

"Probably ran the Grand Canyon a lot, eh?"

"Something like 200 times before he was 18. Hart had himself an Indian girlfriend, and they'd both worked for the raft outfitters since they were kids—you know, setting up camp and cooking and what ·not. Sometimes there wasn't room on the rafts for all the tourists and junk they strap onto them, so Hart started paddling a kayak behind the flotilla. He got to be a legend with those rafters." There was another long pause, and I could hear the coach's rasping breath over the phone. "Kid was only 20 when that fire got him. Nobody will ever know how good he might have become."

Nobody but me, I thought. Whether Edwards and Hart shared a confidence is something I often pondered but never found out, since emphysema carried the old coach away the following Easter.

Several days later, Hank and I spread out the charts and reviewed the topography we'd memorized months before. A thick black line, the Rio Juarez, snaked through the contours passing numerous sections of Piedra Caliza—limestone. The nearest road was a farming track perhaps 10 miles east of the river, so we—or rather Hank—

planned to charter a helicopter in Laredo. The river was in Mexico, where the air space required all kinds of impossible permits, so the pilot would drop us at the mouth of the canyon, just over the border. That meant running the river "blind," without scouting before the big water; which is like marrying a blind date, and having to live or die with whoever turns up. The charts showed no waterfalls, at least. I wouldn't say Hank seemed worried. Concerned, though.

"Good thing we're honed up. This is going to test us," he said, tapping the circuitous black line with his finger. "Second thoughts?"

"None," I lied.

Despite his thirst for violent water, Hank never pushed me into anything. Through all the crazy, seemingly foolhardy stuff we'd done over the last few months, he always ran a grim section first so I could follow his line and would warn me off certain treacherous bits, though he'd normally run them himself. Sometimes he seemed more paranoid about me getting hurt than he was about seeing other people on the water. And his concern about my hide was something beyond just trying to preserve a paddling partner for another run. Life might have taken the heart out of him, but I counted for something nevertheless.

"I'd never try this alone," he said, folding up the map. "You know that."

I asked him if he had any more beer.

"It's not like we *have* to do this."

"We're doing it, Hank."

He shrugged. "I created a frigging monster, here."

"You give yourself too much credit, Hank. I was crazy long before I met you."

"Maybe so." And he smiled truly.

Right then I wanted to lift the veil, to put my talk with coach Edwards out in the open, but the timing was off. I'd know when the moment had come.

We moved from the chart room into one just like it, but with a TV. A Lakers game was on. We lazed around drinking beer and watching the game and barely talked. Hank never said much off the water, anyway, and both our minds were already on the Rio Juarez. But I'd noticed the little framed photo the moment I came into the room, wondering why Hank had it out like that because he was so acutely private about everything. I went over and looked at the photo. Hank said nothing. The only thing I could figure is that he wanted me to see it.

The photo was a Polaroid, and not a very good one. Hank was in a thrashed, fiberglass kayak all painted up with those Navajo designs. Right beside him, hip deep in the muddy water of the lower Colorado, was a girl, her black hair pulled back, her dark eyes locked on Hank. They both looked about 17. Hank had been out in the sun so much he looked almost Navajo himself. There was an eerie sameness about them—something much more than simple affinity—that was unmistakable.

"What was her name?" I finally asked.

"Lucy," he said. He didn't need to tell me she'd been in the car Hank had piled up more than 15 years ago.

We were on the Rio Juarez the following Saturday. From a nearby sandbar, the river's howl drowned out the roar of the chopper, whirring back to the border. At first sight of the river, my heart leapt into my mouth. A breakneck sluice, the torrent rip-roared directly into a gorge before hooking right and disappearing. For several minutes, we just stared. I didn't know water could move so fast. An occasional uprooted oak tore by, barely holding its own above the frothy surface. I kept pushing down the urge to bushwhack out to that farm road 10 miles east.

"Looks like a big sled ride," Hank said, studying the flow.

"Should be OK if we stay centered in the current," I said, trying to believe it. Four months back, I wouldn't have entered that river with a .45 at my temple. We had no idea what lay a quarter mile downstream. Hank shoved his kayak to the water line, slithered in and cinched his spray skirt so taut the draw cord flexed the combing.

"Pull over whenever you can," Hank said, eyes straight ahead. "We've got to scout this one good." I nodded, and tightened my helmet.

We shoved off together. Hank dug a couple deep strokes, and I fell in behind him. When we entered the current, my head snapped back from the speed. Right off I went over, but rolled up OK. We barreled on, knifing through towering rooster tails and haystacks of white water, constantly leaning, bracing, trying to follow the inner flow. The river churned so that the top few feet were cream, so we moved principally on feel. The current eased as we entered the true gorge, limestone slabs angling up sharply from the water line. Then we heard it, around the corner: a low rumble, pulsing between the narrowing canyon walls.

"Get left," shrieked Hank, digging hard across the strong current, his boat lunging with each stroke. No eddies meant no stopping. We turned the corner with our shoulders close to the left wall. Just ahead, the entire left side of the river spun into a hideous whirlpool, the very edge of which swirled clockwise up and off the left-hand wall. A halo of mist revolved around the maw, which gained in size and fury the closer we got. It had to be 30 feet across. No doubt about it, we were heading for a no-exit "keeper" hole from hell.

"Hug the cliff," Hank screamed.

Our chance lay in riding the left-hand lip of the whirlpool, using its downstream momentum to spin us past the cavity. Feeling the circular current yanking me right, I dug my paddle deep left. My boat jumped straight and I caught the white surge flowing off the wall. The force rolled me on edge, the bottom of my boat grinding across the limestone. The mist blinded me, but for one split second the halo parted and I gaped straight into the depths of the gullet, the home of great and grinding boulders. The noise was deafening, the mist thick with the flinty smell of pulverized rock. Just when I thought I might tumble into the eye, my boat slipped down off the wall and I caught the downstream edge of the whirlpool. My bow shot up under the cross current, and I felt it drawing me back in. I teetered, dead in the water, rocking on the very brink.

"Dig!" Hank screamed.

A few atomic strokes put me onto the calm. I screamed until the rock walls trembled, then paddled over to Hank, his face twisted up into that grin of his.

"Buckle up, hombre, we're heading for the Real McCoy."

Below, the river blasted between two walls of living rock that reared vertically off the water. The river bottom was mostly sand because the water ran like glass, though so swift that we covered roughly 15 miles in the next hour (if the topo map was correct). Twice the river pinched to the merest culvert and passed beneath natural bridges; the ceiling on one was only about 5 feet above our heads.

Then the river steepened, rifling us through a slalom course of rock pinnacles sprouting from the water like great tenpins on end. From each side of these leapt treacherous wakes, requiring all my expertise running gates to avoid them. Twice the wakes flipped me, and twice I barely avoided a grievous head-on. Smacking a pinnacle might not have iced me outright, but it would have demolished the boat and I would have drowned in spite of my life jacket. There was no shoreline to grope for, no alcove to hide in. When we finally pulled into calm waters, we'd been toiling full bore for more than two hours. We stroked over left to a thank-God shelf, dragged our boats onto it and collapsed.

Hank had smacked the canyon wall hard enough to cost him the left arm of his wet suit, and he had a nasty rake across the forearm. I'd struck so much debris that my boat leaked slightly from half a dozen spots. From the second we'd entered the canyon there was no going back and no getting out. A look downstream would have turned the stomach of a statue.

One hundred yards below, the river plunged and accelerated into a boiling rage that seemed too savage for rock to contain. Fifty yards farther down, the canyon pitched like a ski jump before hooking sharply left. At the elbow, the entire river dashed 40 feet up the right wall and formed a seething, tsunami-sized perpetual wave with a nimbus of vapors swirling above it.

"Look at that," Hank yelled. A huge log torpedoed past. Stripped bald from its rugged passage, it resembled a giant white bone bobbing atop the whitewater. It disappeared, then popped back up just before the elbow. My guts turned to water as it arced 40 feet up and 60 feet across the perpetual wave. At the wave's cresting apex, it tumbled down, end over end, and was washed around the corner.

Staring at that tumbling log, I had the sinking feeling that my plans for the future had sustained me all along, that my paddling was only a dodge to push those plans aside and that shortly I would come clean, find a proper woman and settle down—which I wanted more than all the rivers on all the maps. And I knew those plans would never make it past that wave. Most likely I didn't want those things at all, just a corner of me was screaming louder than the rest. But the moment ruined me, and I sat there dashed and remote. I would have prayed to God if I hadn't hated him so much.

"You see that?" Hank screamed, citing the huge log. "Hell, we can *make* this. The water's so high it'll flush us right through so long as we stay centered in the current. But we've got to come in low on that wave. That's for sure." Hank cinched the strap on his helmet and started for his boat. "No good just staring at it, John."

But I might as well have been part of the rock I was sitting on. Hank was setting out to tackle something that combined a 40-foot Makaha wave with a section of Niagara Falls, but none of that mattered and it never had. He'd try the unthinkable because only after he'd slipped through another terminal rapid did he feel that his life was worth living. Then he'd start spiraling down to zero again, and it was back to insane water, then back to zero and it was just one endless, crazy go-around. But it had to end somewhere. One look downriver told me where.

Hank grabbed my arm, and said, "I'm scared, John. Hell yes, I am. But we're going to make this. Believe it."

I had to believe him, or try to convince myself I believed him because I could no more claw over those sheer wet walls and escape the canyon than I could paddle back upriver. The only way out was over that perpetual wave. And the Holy Ghost couldn't survive that wave.

"We're never going to make this," I said.

For the briefest moment Hank seemed ready to admit it, that we were finished. But he caught himself at last, and said nothing.

"I guess it doesn't matter to someone whose got nothing to lose," I added.

"I've got you to lose. So quit acting like you're not worth saving."

"Fuck you," I said, glaring back at him. The thunderous water below felt like it was rushing through the middle of me.

We stood glaring at each other—or rather, I glared and Hank looked away. I felt small, because before we ever set foot in Mexico, Hank had said we didn't have to run this river at all, and I insisted that we did. And yet, I also felt betrayed because in the first place, Hank's compulsion to escape the wreckage of his life had drawn me into a river of no return. This was unfair to Hank, but my blood still boiled to see him count on my readiness to follow him into the next world. I slouched back on the rock and tried to steady up and even forget, but all I could think about were Hank's early morning phone calls and his fumbling to reach out to me, and the plain fact that I would never meet that good woman now and that we were both dust, and all of this made the situation pitiful.

"This is no way for two friends to handle a minor obstacle," Hank said.

"Minor?" I said, looking downstream. "You got to risk your life to save it, fair enough. But paddling into *that*—shit, Hank. We're just tossing ours away."

"How can you say that about something you've never even tried?"

"I've never tried blowing my brains out, neither, but I can reckon the outcome if I did. Look at that thing. *Listen* to it." We were 150 yards away from the worst of it and it still sounded like an Apollo rocket lifting off. The notion of intentionally paddling into that chaos sickened me, more because I had no choice but to do it. We fell back into silence again. I should have hauled out my conversation with Coach Edwards and confronted Ronnie Hart himself, but in dangerous situations you think only of yourself and I wasn't worried about anything but my next breath.

Hank moved about 10 feet away, sat down and stared grimly into a patch of calm water below us. The torment he stoically bore all those years looked to be pushing him into the rock. He surely knew he was finally up against it, and the way he sat there with a numb look on his face, watching the river, I thought maybe he might dive into the current and be done with the whole business. But slowly, as I studied him with a sort of morbid intrigue, I realized—or thought I realized—that he wasn't brooding or groveling at all, rather focusing on what had to be done. And that's what, in a terrible kind of way, made the guy so magnificent, this brute resolve to push beyond the memories to the rapids beyond. That he could never push completely free was beside the point. The marvel was that he didn't know but to try, and to try the faith of a falling man lunging for a cobweb. It was all a kind of madness, of course, and as usual, a tiny bit of it slowly rubbed off on me. After a couple minutes, I asked, "You think we got any chance at all here?"

"I do," he said, turning toward me and flashing that sly grin of his.

"Well anything's better than sitting here looking at it." We silently got back into our kayaks, secured the spray skirts and paddled over to the far right. Danger and delight grew on one stalk for Hank, and even now he acted like our fortune was assured. I felt that if I had to die, paddling straight into the teeth of it was as good a way as any.

We hit the current, and were off.

Vaulting toward the bend, I saw that Hank—just ahead—came in too high as he charged onto the perpetual wave. He sliced across, suddenly dragged his right blade and shot up to the crest. Momentarily weightless, he dug his right blade deep: the stern of his boat slid around, and he shot down the wave—backward, but perfectly aligned. Now facing me, Hank plunged down off the wave and into the cataract before us, that inimitable grin all over his face. Then I too dove into the falls and was swallowed.

Locked inside the plunging tube, I fell for what seemed like minutes. The impact ripped me from my boat, and the falls drove me to the bottom and pinned me there face down, like a pinioned stag. Then I was dashed around and my limbs felt like they were being ripped off my body. I surfaced facing the falls, where wakes swamped me over and over. Without a life jacket, I would have been gone. Limp and gasping, I bobbed into calm waters. I spotted Hank downstream, an arm draped over each boat, retching up half the river. But his hacking soon turned to howling. I struggled over to the boats, draped my arms over the bow, and blew about a pint of water out of my sinuses.

"I defy you to find a tougher run!" Hank wailed.

"I don't want to," I coughed out.

"That's it. The ultimate—no one can top it," he rambled on.

"I'll never try, I promise you."

"And you took the easy way...." Hank's grin confirmed what I hadn't had time to think through: that he'd intentionally lined up high on the wave and had taken on the falls—backward. And what finally surfaced from the spume was not a fugitive, not a snake-bitten loner, but a kid from an old Polaroid picture. I knew no matter what might happen the rest of the day, Hank could never tumble all the way back down to zero. Later, perhaps. For sure he would. But not that day. That day was his. Was ours.

We kicked over to the narrow shore, dumped the water from our boats and lay back. Both kayaks were thrashed, and I wished we'd taken the plastic ones instead of the fiberglass boats, which were lighter and faster but fragile in comparison. I noted the last run had ground the little Navajo design off Hank's boat. No matter. Hank kept blubbering and slapping my back in a way I would have sworn was impossible 30 minutes earlier. I was tempted to reveal my secret, but Hank was so high that I didn't want to risk pulling him back down.

Until then, I didn't fully realize how lucky we were because I'd been fretting so hard over trying to survive—or rather, about the fact that we were positively going to die. Now I felt released from some very dark jaws. Though the soggy map showed more limestone below, we had quit the narrowest canyon, and by all indications had only 20 miles of easier river to reach El Estribo, the "Stirrup," a town of 9,000.

We'd planned on two days, but it was only mid-afternoon, so we pushed on. I felt half-dead, but snapped to at the first white water, where Hank clowned through 15-foot combers. The guy was paddling a hundred miles above the water.

Then the river suddenly dropped, charging on with the same fury it had above the falls. We cranked around a bend, and just before us, the entire river flowed straight into a mountainside. Of course, it went under this buttress, but the only visible breach was a tiny chink, dead center, looking like a doghouse door as we hurtled toward it. This all happened faster than I could panic, and I reflexively lined up behind Hank. Twenty feet before the wall, I saw the chink was wide enough, but would clip our heads off. Hank suddenly rolled upside down and knifed into the crack just as I flipped over.

Blazing down a swift river, upside down, inside a mountain, is a sensation I won't try and describe. Fearing I'd get my head torn off if I rolled back up, I stayed upside down until my lungs caught fire. I rolled up only to carom off a wall and plunge down again. Whatever I hit demolished my boat and pitched me head over heels through the darkness. Finally belched out of the mountain into calm but swift-moving water, I didn't know who or where I was and for several minutes bobbed around in a carbonated pool. Slowly my head cleared. Facing the buttress rising out of the river, the water churned and gurgled from the bowels of the rock like a torrent from a giant storm grate. I couldn't see where I'd come out. Under the waterline, somewhere. I spun around and dog-paddled through fragments of our splintered boats, floating around me. I was scrapped and battered but otherwise unhurt, still clutching my unbroken paddle. Beyond me, the river crept through open Savannah. The difficulties were all behind us now. But where was Hank? Then I spotted him, floating by the right bank. He didn't move as I stroked over to him. He was conscious, though dazed. I grabbed the collar of his life jacket and dragged him onto shore.

I felt around for broken bones, and when I rolled him over, I nearly puked. Two daggers of fiberglass were sunk deep into his back. I drew out the first one, maybe four inches long, directly from his spine. Hank's legs twitched for a second, then went dead. When I removed an even bigger shard from his side, blood gushed out and nothing I could do would stop it. The guy was going to die on me then and there, though I wouldn't admit it to myself. I dragged Hank onto a little rock bench and sat him upright. Only then did I see that blood from a head gash had drained into his eyes.

"Can you get my eyes?" Hank asked calmly. "I can't move my arms." He looked pale. I wiped his eyes.

"You've got some deep wounds in your back, Hank, but we'll just rest up a bit and take it from there."

"I'm history, John. I can't even feel my body." I couldn't say anything, and must have looked hysterical.

"Relax," he reassured me. I couldn't look at him just then. When I could, he flashed me that grin of his.

"These last few months have meant something to me, John. You're the best paddler I've ever seen."

"I'm nothing compared to you, Mr. Ronnie Hart."

He coughed out a chuckle.

"I called old Edwards and he told me everything. Even how you crushed Accomazzo in Italy."

"He wouldn't have made it 10 feet down this river."

"Ronnie, you could have been world champ for 20 years. And I should know, because I was the champion for three."

"Sounds good to hear my name." I wiped the blood from his eyes again. "I never really cared about running gates and all that. That was never kayaking to me. What mattered was big water, and we ran the biggest."

"Ronnie, nobody will ever repeat what we've done—ever."

"I won't say never, but we were first."

"You were first, Ronnie. I always followed your lead."

We talked quietly for another 10 minutes. I promised to keep Ronnie's secret, and to bury him next to the river. His voice waned to a whisper, and though he couldn't raise an arm, his courage never flagged. Smiling slightly, the great Ronnie Hart melded with the purring current and slowly floated away. It all happened so fast.

I broke my paddle in half and used it to dig into the moist soil. In an hour, I laid Ronnie Hart to rest, where his soul could hear the rapids roll so long as the river flowed. As I heaped the ground upon him, I tried to say something pious, but I wasn't making any sense so I finally quit trying. Still, it was right, me fumbling for a few words, and it was right and fitting that Ronnie had died there. The future held nothing for him. He would never get any higher than he'd been that day, nor would he ever live down his past. For a few brief hours the river had taken him back to a time he'd never wanted to leave. Now, he would never have to. I threw the broken paddles in the river and watched them drift into the night. I had nothing left.

The book had slammed shut on Ronnie Hart, and the fitting end was there, on the river. Unfortunately, I had to get off the river and out of Mexico. I collapsed on shore that night, watched a cold moon inch across the sky, and arose battered, stiff and exhausted. And starving. I took a compass bearing due east and set off, hoping to gain the farm road in half a day, terrain permitting.

It didn't.

After cresting a hill, the wet dirt turned to mud, ankle deep for a mile, then knee deep for two more. I had to plow a trough through the ooze. The sun beat down, and I kept thinking the mud would turn to quicksand. About noon, the mud gave way to waist-high thicket, each branch bristling with hooked thorns. No use trying to avoid the barbs, since getting free from one meant getting snagged by another. Within 10 minutes thorns were tearing straight through my wetsuit and into my flesh. Soon, the shrub grew so thick that I had to drag myself over the top on all fours. Branches snapped, dropping me into thorns that slashed my face and arms. My wetsuit hung in bloody tatters. I was so weary I could barely focus on my compass. Every time I tried to move on hunch, I found myself going in circles. Hours later, I stumbled across a stagnant creek. I was too exhausted to move, much less continue, but the bugs were fearsome and swarmed about my wounds. To escape them, I groveled into the black water, set my head on the rocky bank, and passed out. By morning, the mosquitoes had nearly closed both my eyes.

I pushed on, weak and stumbling. The ground was riven with little trenches that I would tumble into and exhaust myself trying to claw out of. My throat burned, and it took everything I had to read the compass. I would close my eyes, concentrate, then quickly glance down before the needle would fuzz and dance. I entered a half-mile stretch of putrid quagmire, passed by half-swimming, half-fording through the thick green soup. Every time I touched a log I thought it was a crocodile or something worse, and I struck out with fresh vigor. The final bog ended at a clay bank. But every time I tried to climb out the lip mushed away, pitching me back into the mire. The reeking water felt like acid on my wounds.

I gave up many times.

On flat ground at last, I crawled under a tree and lay breathless in meager shade. Voices came from nearby, and I looked up and saw—or thought I saw—two men on mules. But I was too wasted to hail them. I must have passed out. When I came to, I spent my last energies crawling over to the road, maybe 50 yards. Of the next few hours I remember only fragments: a sunset, an oxcart, a bumpy ride and a candle flickering in an adobe hovel.

I came around to find an old Indian woman digging thorns from my nakedness with a dull pin. An old man handed me a wineskin of water and I guzzled it in one long draw. My hands were so torn and swollen I couldn't have even held a kayak paddle—and I never would again. I spent the next day dozing and eating while the old woman applied red mud paddies and caustic herbs to my wounds. I never understood a thing she or the old man said, so I couldn't convey my nightmare. Maybe that was better, because from then on, Ronnie's death was strictly my own affair. The next day they hitched up the cart and took me to a highway near the border. I've always meant to go back and thank them. Maybe someday I will.

La Bohn Gap

By Jonathan M. Karpoff

The pirate looked at me in amazement: "You went up to Chain Lakes through the Necklace Valley? And you lived?" She sounded genuinely amazed. "Most people get there through Dutch Miller Gap!"

It's Halloween, and the spooks are out, I thought. At least, this woman is giving me the spooks. She said her name was Jenny. I had never met her before, but even if I had, I would not have been able to tell. It was a masquerade party and her costume was, well, effective. She had the standard pirate paraphernalia: eye patch, a red-and-white striped bandanna, and a menacing dagger strapped to her belt like an open dare to any man thinking about inviting her to dance to the rumba music blaring on the stereo. But I barely noticed any of this. I could not take my eyes off of two things: the fake (I hoped) scar oozing blood so realistically from Jenny's thigh, and the fact that, in her torn pirate costume, I could see Jenny's thigh.

So when we had met five minutes before, Jenny was very cool and imposing. But we soon discovered a common interest—hiking in Washington's Cascade Mountains—and she warmed to the topic. We swapped stories on places we had been until, like a secret password, I mentioned that I had been up around La Bohn Gap and some nearby pools called Chain Lakes. That's when Jenny momentarily forgot that she was the coolest person in the room, and gave me the largest, if unwarranted, compliment I had received in a long time.

"Jeez, that is one difficult way to get in there..." Jenny was saying, still buttering me up. I couldn't understand why she was making a big deal about it. After all, the route I had followed was a no-brainer. It even had a trail most of the way. I did not think I had done anything to merit such praise.

Then Jenny dropped the bomb. "You know," she said, "the USGS map has La Bohn Gap in the wrong place."

It all made sense now. Not Jenny's adulation, which still seemed exaggerated, but 10 weeks of head-scratching. An old Alaskan sourdough once claimed, "I ain't never been lost. But I sure have been confused a few times." Well, I had been confused near La Bohn Gap weeks before, and had been puzzled ever since. In a flash, with

Jenny's comment about the USGS map being wrong, my puzzle was solved....

My buddy, John, and I made camp in the Necklace Valley surrounded by lakes that had once made someone think of a string of pearls. We argued about the valley's name while we heated water and swatted bugs. John was not impressed by two of the lakes we had passed, calling them "mudholes." Geez, I thought, give it a break. I thought the setting was stunning.

It would have been more stunning, however, if the clouds would part and stop dripping on us. Maybe John was grouchy because of the lousy weather. We convinced ourselves that the next day would be better, that the sun would shine and warm us, and that we would have terrific views from the top of Mount Hinman, a broad sugarloaf of a mountain, offering an afternoon saunter along a western ridge that skirts above north-facing glaciers.

John, ever the grouch, called it "Mount Himmler." I put up with this moaning because Hinman seemed the perfect mountain for us: it was easy. In addition, we had a route description from one of Fred Beckey's guidebooks. Beckey, a legendary climber, is the author of three climbing guidebooks for Washington's Cascade Mountains. Today, few people head for any Cascade peak without first checking Beckey's route descriptions. Some people call the books "Beckey's Bibles," and the plaudit is well-earned. Little did we know that, in our neophyte hands and on Mount Himmler, Beckey's Bibles could be dangerous.

The next morning part of our wish was granted—the rain had stopped. But the clouds hung low as we pushed up toward Mount Hinman—or Himmler—via La Bohn Gap. Beckey's book is clear on what to do:

"From La Bohn Gap ascend talus and slopes (keep left of broad west ridge) half mile east to the ridge which runs northeast at 6,600 feet. Ascend this easy ridge (it crests along the top of the Hinman Glacier) and then east to the summit."

This made no sense to us. The map indicated that straight east of La Bohn Gap was a precipitous 1,100-foot drop to Lake Rowena. Nonetheless, Fred Beckey said to start from La Bohn Gap, so that is what we were going to do. Besides, the pea-soup fog refused to let up, pretty much preventing any freelancing. We could see our map and compass. We could see our photocopy of Beckey's route description. But we could see little else. Boulders and hillocks invisible at 75 feet loomed out of the fog when we got within 50 feet.

To get to where the map says La Bohn Gap is, we hiked to a broad saddle at 5,900 feet, then dropped down and south onto a 5,500-foot granite bench containing a series of potholes called Chain Lakes. We then turned east to scamper up a high narrow saddle prominently titled "La Bohn Gap" on the map. Here, at Beckey's starting point, we finally had to face the inconsistency between the map and his route description. He said to go east. But, just as the map indicated, east led straight down—*straight down!*

What to do? We clearly were at La Bohn Gap, right where the map said. But we also knew we could not go east as Beckey instructed. East meant down the cliff. And somewhere through the fog at the bottom of the cliff lay Lake Rowena, not Mount Himmler.

Then, in a moment of proof that two heads are not necessarily better than one, we came upon a solution: perhaps Beckey meant *north*, not east! Heck, we all know the caprice of editors and typesetters. Some deskbound lout probably inserted "east" into the text between bites of his pastrami-on-rye, thus changing Beckey's directions. Lesser climbers might not figure out such a screwup, we thought. We, gonzo mountaineers, were not so easily put off. Inserting the word "north" where the text said "east" solved our problem.

Or so we thought. For the next 30 minutes, we prided ourselves on the brilliance of our solution. We picked our way across a broad talus slope, hopping from rock to rock like kids at a park. Then two things happened that whitened my hair. First, I kicked off a rock that skipped down the slope out of view into the thick fog—*and I did not hear it land.* Second, the clouds parted enough to show me why. A golden ray of sun shone 50 feet below me and to my right. It shone into nothingness. It shone all the way down to Lake Rowena. *Straight* down.

That moment of sunshine illuminated our situation, but I did not like what I saw. We were traversing a broad cirque hanging over a 500-foot cliff band above Lake Rowena. It was like traveling across the inside of a gigantic cereal bowl. The sides of the bowl, however, were covered with rocks shaped like large granola cereal nuggets, some of which were sliding down into the pool at the bowl's middle. Our goal was now clear. We had to get to the other side of the bowl without triggering an avalanche of gigantic granola-like rocks that would carry us down into the pool below.

John also saw the abyss below us. We looked at each other and, without words, spread the distance between us, moved uphill and stopped playing around. We kicked off several more tiny rock avalanches. Each time, the rocks tumbled out of sight into the fog and were silenced as they swung over the cliff's edge.

It was at about this time that a crack appeared in John's and my theory of Beckey's screwed-up directions. "Keep left of broad west ridge," Beckey warned. In rationalizing the discrepancy between Beckey's directions and the map, we conveniently had ignored this warning. Now I realized that we were not to the left of anything, except the empty space above Lake Rowena. We were, however, to the *right* of a ridge which, the map said, leads north and then northeast toward the summit. Maybe, I hoped, there were two typos in the route description. Maybe Beckey meant, "Keep to the *right* of the broad west ridge," as John and I now were. But I realized that this was more hope than reason.

We reached the ridge top, then followed it. Now things felt right, since this is what Beckey's directions said to do. I did not look forward to our return traverse on the slope above Lake Rowena, but by this time I had convinced myself that we had deciphered Beckey's directions correctly enough, and that any alternate route must be worse.

On our return, however, my partner's better sense finally kicked into gear. From the ridge top above Lake Rowena, I motioned that we should head back the way we had come.

"No way," said John. "I'm not going back that way."

This seemed foolish to me. Maybe John was still grumpy about the crummy weather. "Come on," I said. "We'll get back to camp before it gets dark if we simply retrace our steps."

"I don't care," said the grump. "I'm not going back across that slope."

We had a problem on our hands, and stopped to argue. I claimed that we at least knew there were no impasses the way we had come. Furthermore, we knew the route and would not have to stop periodically to check our location and direction. John refused to budge. I argued that Beckey's directions, as we had deciphered them, had a rhyme and reason. There must be something even worse ahead if we tried to alter our course. John responded that Beckey's directions made sense only because we kept inserting our own words into them. I responded with ironclad logic, and called John a chicken. Even this didn't work. So, finally, instead of turning south and heading across the cereal bowl above Lake Rowena, we turned west into the unknown cliffs hidden by the impenetrable fog.

We did indeed find cliffs. I now suspect there are not many cliffs on that northwest slope of Mount Hinman's west ridge. But however many there are, we found them all. One after another, we stumbled into an impasse, climbed back upslope and worked down another way. We spent a lot of time peering into the fog and imagining things. On at least three occasions, I was sure that I could see La Bohn Lakes, a landmark we passed on our way up in the morning. Each time, however, my vision of the lakes disintegrated into nothingness as the light shifted through the fog. Snowfields below us appeared like holes in the mountainside, suggesting impassable cliffs. And real holes in the mountain appeared only meters before we stepped into them. It definitely was not a good day for glissading down the snowfields.

It was during one of our stops to scratch our heads and figure things out that John spotted something unexpected: "Hey, there's a trail!" I peered through the fog with skepticism. But, sure enough, there it was. Not a regular trail maintained with shovels and picks. Not much more than a path for springwater runoff. But, clearly, a previously trodden path angling downslope. This was welcome news, but still confusing. We were supposed to be on the wrong side of the ridge, the side Beckey warned us to stay off. But here was a trail. Clearly, somebody, or lots of somebodies, had been on this side of the ridge. What was going on?

We lost the trail and picked it up again several times. But it did not matter. By now we were off the rocks and on gentle heather slopes. We found several landmarks we had passed on the way up, and in short order were back in camp. As night overcame the fog, we drank quarts of hot cocoa and took turns belting out show tunes. Somehow, our easy trek had turned into an adventure, and we had returned safely. We were triumphant.

The puzzling inconsistencies remained, however. Why did Beckey's directions say to go east from La Bohn Gap, instead of north? Why did it say to stay to the left of the west ridge, instead of right? Why were there well-beaten boot tracks on our return path, when we were groping our way down the mountain?

I stared at Jenny the pirate with the stunned look that comes from sudden revelation. "Say that again?" I asked, even though I had heard her clearly the first time.

"What?" she said. "Oh, you mean that the USGS map has La Bohn Gap in the wrong place?"

I did not need to ask how she knew, or on what authority she could make such a claim. I knew immediately that she was right. I also did not need to ask where the real La Bohn Gap is. I knew that too—immediately. The answers to my questions became apparent, the puzzles that had pestered me from the moment I had stared after the rock I had kicked into the abyss over Lake Rowena.

The place the USGS map labels "La Bohn Gap" is a minor saddle, two-thirds of a mile southeast of the real La Bohn Gap. We had traveled over the real La Bohn Gap—it's the broad saddle at 5,900 feet from which we dropped into Chain Lakes. The real La Bohn Gap is due west of Hinman's broad west ridge. From it, Beckey's directions make sense: Travel east for a half mile, staying to the left of the west ridge, then turning northeast along the top of the ridge.

That means that on our way up, John and I were on the wrong side of the ridge! And on the way down, we stumbled onto the normal route as described in Beckey's book! John, my grumpy, chicken partner, was correct to keep us off the slope above Lake Rowena. His obstinance led us to the gentle footpaths tread by other, less confused hikers.

Jenny the pirate was staring at me and saying something. I heard little, and for the first time since meeting her did not have to work to keep my eyes off her costume. In one statement, she had solved 10 weeks of a nagging puzzle. Perhaps I should have felt embarrassed not to have figured out the map's error myself. But I didn't.

Thanks, Jenny.

I Should've Worn Wranglers

By Michael Hodgson

As we tumbled out of the van squinting through settling road dust and wrinkling our noses at the musty smell of sage, we were greeted by the spittin' image of Pecos Bill—had to be him. His boyish smile peeked out from behind the strands of a mustache gone wild while eyes steeled by years of cowboying and guiding sized us up from beneath the shadow of a dusty cowboy hat—pulled low and tight on his head. He walked with a slight swagger, exaggerated perhaps because of the fit of his boots, meant for riding, not striding, and his spurs jingled with each step. Well-worn leather chaps with stains and smudges that could have been blood, could have been trail dirt, hung low on his narrow hips. His skin was well-tanned and as he stuck his trail-worn hand out to shake mine, he introduced himself as Al, Al Brown—so much for my Pecos Bill fantasy.

As Al and Polly Gogins, his partner at All 'Round Ranch gathered us around, he began the introductions by announcing that "any fool person can gallop on a horse, but it takes a skilled rider to know how to control that horse."

Well, that about counted me out. My only experience on horseback had been several months earlier during an adventure race called the Eco-Challenge. I had only ridden six times prior to then, garnering a grand total of six hours of equestrian experience—a few hours shy of being able to swagger like a cowboy, but long enough to know that horses and I keep separate company for good reason. During the race, I was bucked, stepped on and had my backside generally beaten to a pulp by a ragged-looking horse who seemed hell bent on making life miserable for anyone who got near him. There was no way I was ever getting on a horse again!

Of course, I suffer from an affliction common to many adventurers known as short-term memory loss, because when an opportunity came along weeks later to ride horses with my 12-year-old daughter, Nicole, I jumped at it. One week in the saddle on the high desert along the Colorado/Utah border. I thought "great adventure, good story material, how bad could it possibly be...," the dull residual ache in the seat of my pants notwithstanding.

I tuned back into Al who was at this point announcing that he had read all of our application forms, along with the personality profiles we filled out, and was going to partner each of us to a horse in his herd with a similar personality—matchmaking cowboy style.

Al must have been reading my application upside down. What I clearly required was an older horse with a penchant for moving slowly and taking care of his rider. Instead, I got Rowdy—a young quarter horse full of spirit with rockets for legs. In fact, Rowdy had won the national championship in arena racing just the week prior, setting a national record along the way. I'm not sure if Al realized he had just tossed a set of Ferrari keys to a driver who probably couldn't even qualify for a learner's permit.

My daughter, an experienced equestrian, had no such trepidation. In fact, although her horse, Concho, a paint quarter horse, clearly outweighed her by 10,000 to one, she couldn't have been happier. Galloping through knee-high sage and zig-zagging among herds of snorting cattle was her dream come true. Whether Dad lived through the experience was, at this point, inconsequential.

There's more to riding than just mounting up and hanging on for a wild ride as I was to quickly discover. Although I'd signed up for a dude ranch experience in one sense, the ranch's operational roots can be traced to Al's past as a regional director for Outward Bound. That meant I could forget sitting around drinking beers and waiting for a saddled horse to be led to my easy chair. All 'Round Ranch's philosophy is about encouraging its buckaroos to become all around riders; able to take care of themselves, their horses, group chores, and push personal boundaries in the process. Hell, I was pushing personal boundaries just trying to pull on my cowboy boots without losing my balance. But, that wasn't enough for them. They wanted to challenge me further by making me responsible for the care of a horse for a week. Jeez, I really should have worn Wranglers.

Every morning, for the next five days, the routine was the same. I'd stagger out of my teepee, trying not to trip over my sleeping daughter. Then I'd slip into my nylon adventure pants and travel shirt, pull on my cowboy boots, top the ensemble off with a canvas hat, and stumble to the mess tent for my morning elixir—cowboy coffee with enough caffeine to knock a mule head over heels across the widest prairie. Following several mugs of liquid breakfast, I'd grab a halter, enter the arena and work my way through the herd trying to locate Rowdy. The next 10 minutes would be spent in a negotiation with my horse, trying to convince him that it was really going to be a good idea to let me slip the halter around his neck and lead him out of the arena so I could saddle him up and go riding for the day.

I am sure this was all great fun for Rowdy. He'd let me get close, carefully watching me while munching on his breakfast of fresh hay. Then just as I was about to place the halter around his neck, he'd casually lean away, sidestep, whirl and flick my face with his tail before sauntering off for a bit more roughage. He'd always stop after a few feet, of course, just to taunt me. He'd grab another mouthful of hay, cock his head, give me a sideways glance that seemed to say, "Come on, let's do that halter thing again," and then begin to chew, slowly. Finally, after playing this game for 10 minutes, he'd tire, or take pity, and allow me to secure the halter and lead him out to the side of the corral for his daily curry combing, vet checking, hoof picking and saddling.

Curry combing and vet checking wasn't so bad, but picking hooves was dirty, strenuous work and not for the faint of heart. Hanging onto the 500-pound leg of an animal who could, if it didn't like how I was probing around its hindquarters and hoof, kick me end-over-end through the distant outhouse requires more than a little confidence. Still, there was something tremendously satisfying about it all—the smell of leather, sweat and grime mingling with the perfume of early morning air carried across the Blue Mountain plateau on gentle breezes.

Rowdy, bless his little heart, always managed to add his own music and perfume to the early morning by choosing to blow wind anytime I was working near his backside. I noticed that none of the other buckaroos, including my daughter, were having problems with gaseous equines. Of course, I also noticed I was the only one wearing nylon adventure pants and not jeans. Apparently, Rowdy was just showing his disdain for anyone who didn't have enough self-respect to at least try to look like a cowboy. I really should have worn Wranglers.

On my first ride, I got a taste for what Rowdy could do. We were heading back to camp when Polly decided to guide our group down a shortcut. To this greenhorn's eyes, the shortcut resembled a cliff that needed a ladder or at the very least, stairs. No matter. Polly headed over the edge and down a strip of dirt that could only loosely be described as a trail. I harkened back to Al's words of advice to me before we headed out.

"Take care of Rowdy and he'll take care of you...go light on the bit, gentle on the reins."

Leaning way back in my saddle and reminding myself that I hadn't heard of any journalist getting killed on an adventure assignment yet this year, I headed Rowdy downhill. As we skidded, skipped and stutter-stepped our way down, I began to realize that the more I relaxed, the more Rowdy took control and the more secure I felt. So that's what Al meant. Now, if I could convince my butt cheeks to quit hanging onto the saddle for dear life, I might actually begin to look relaxed.

That night, Al called me out in front of the group for my taste in cowboy fashion, or, in his eyes, lack of taste. "What's with the hat? Couldn't you find a decent cowboy hat?"

"It's my favorite hat Al...been with me through thick and thin."

Al squinted into the firelight, picked his nails with a knife, then fired off another round.

"Real cowboys wear cotton, wool and leather...what the heck kind of pants are those?"

"Ex Officio—best adventuring pants I've ever owned."

Al rolled his eyes, pursed his lips and exhaled slowly, with obvious disdain. "Real cowboys wear Wranglers..."

I noticed a tiny revolver handle showing itself, sticking ever so slightly out of small pouch on Al's chaps just below his left hip. I wondered aloud about its purpose.

"It's for putting a horse or cow down if it's got a broken leg...we don't want anything to suffer out here," Al drawled. While he seemed sincere with his explanation, the glint in his eyes told me he just might use it on greenhorns who didn't dress the cowboy way— God, I wish I'd worn Wranglers.

With a thousand or more stars painting the midnight sky, Nik and I headed to bed.

"Dad?"

"Yes."

"I want to work for All 'Round Ranch when I get older."

I couldn't shake that infernal song, "Mothers (dads), don't let your sons (daughters) grow up to be cowboys" from the dusty recesses of my head as I slipped off to sleep.

Two days later, following an all-day shakeout ride, a midmorning sun chased us up Meadow Creek, across the Vincent Ranch and onto Joe Hacking's school section pasture. Until now, we had been learning and playing. Today we worked. Hidden down in one of the narrow canyons lined with shimmering aspen and tangled sage was an injured black heifer with hoof rot. Al had been treating her and needed to give her a checkup along with another injection of antibiotic and force sulfa tablets down her throat.

As we wound down into the canyon, ducking under branches that threatened to peel an unsuspecting rider right off his saddle, we began to hear bugling. Elk. Hundreds of them all around us. Mothers with calves, young bulls and a few older bulls with elegant racks all scattered, leaping and jumping through the underbrush in a quest for higher ground and safety that the ridge above promised them.

Rowdy slipped sideways and shuffled down a steep slope of loose rocks and rubble all the way to the canyon floor where he jumped a stream with elegant grace—elegant right up to the point when I smacked back into the saddle with a jaw shattering thud. Rowdy glanced over his shoulder in my direction and snorted, loudly. "Work with me, babe," he seemed to be saying. Al looked my way, too.

"Al, if I live through this, I'm going straight to the nearest store to procure a pair of Wranglers...honest!" I'm not sure if he bought it or not, but it seemed to make Rowdy happy.

The underbrush along the canyon floor was dense, making the search for the black heifer difficult. I pointed out numerous cows, none of which was the right one—heck, they all looked the same to me. Nik and Marne, a 14-year-old girl also on the trip with as much passion for horses as my daughter, both yelled at the same time, "There she is!"

Scott blazed by, rope snaked out in a large, lazy loop circling over his head as he guided his horse in and out of the trees, leaning this way and that. Al and Polly also began the chase while I worked on just trying to stay out of the way. Cutting close to the heifer, Scott expertly flicked his wrist and laid his rope neatly out and around...yep, a bush. Damn! Rocks and dirt flew as he skidded to a power stop. Al cut in behind. The heifer was running for her proverbial life. She must have thought hell and damnation just rode down out of the sky behind her. Al snapped his rope around the heifer's hind leg, pulling her up short. Polly, right alongside dropped her rope around the heifer's neck and pulled tightly. The heifer lunged, jerking PJ, Polly's horse off his feet, over backward and onto Polly—suddenly, it was horse riding rider. Dust and snot were flying, Al was yelling, Polly scrambled to her feet and PJ decided it would be a good time to fall down on Polly again. Fortunately, Polly averted disaster with a quick sidestep.

With the heifer now controlled by two ropes, Nik and Marne leapt from their saddles and dove on top of the heifer to wrestle it down— 170 pounds trying to sit on 800. Within five minutes, it was all over. The heifer was going to be fine and her hoof was healing nicely. Released, she scrambled to her feet and ran off. We headed back to camp, trotting all the way.

Trotting is a painful gait to sit as it's bounce, bounce, bounce. Walking, as Al put it, is just too slow for a real cowboy, you never get anywhere. Galloping and loping are fine for short bursts, but they'll wear your mount out in no time. So, to get anywhere in a reasonable amount of time, you trot. For me, riding the trot had become a matter of pure survival: Slap, slap, bounce, owww, damn, slap, slap, find the rhythm, ahhh, lose the rhythm, and slap, slap, again. My butt and knees began to hate life.

Scott, mercifully, rode up beside me.

"Drop your heels, relax your shoulders and sit lower in the saddle."

I did.

"Now, relax and concentrate on feeling your horse's rhythm and watching his shoulders. Each time he steps, you place weight on your stirrup on the side he is stepping on—it's a bit like dancing, only your horse is leading and you're following."

So, I began to dance. It didn't take long until I began to feel like a regular Fred Astaire, though I'm not sure Rowdy would appreciate being likened to Ginger Rogers.

I was sitting taller in the saddle now, I could feel it. As we headed off to a new camp the following day, we drove a herd of cattle ahead of us, moving them to a new watering hole. Rowdy and I began working together. He was still very much the teacher, but I was less the unsure student. We spotted several cows wandering away from the herd along a ridge several hundred yards distant. Leaning forward in the saddle and giving Rowdy a squeeze with my legs and heels, we blasted off in their direction. I clung onto the saddle horn to keep my balance as Rowdy surged over the tops of sage bushes and nimbly placed his feet down on the rugged terrain. For a moment, as I relaxed my grip on the saddle horn, unclenched butt cheeks from their tenuous hold on saddle leather, and stood slightly in the stirrups, I felt the glorious ecstasy of flying. All I had to do was touch the reins to either side of Rowdy's neck and he turned. As we flanked the wayward cows, I sat back and Rowdy slowed. Slapping my hand to my thigh and yelling, "Yahh, yahh," we headed the runaways back to the main herd. My imagination drifted—I was a young lad on the set with John Wayne in the movie *Cowboys*, living a dream. Nothing could be more perfect.

Later that afternoon, as we sat high in the saddle on the lip of a canyon overlooking the Yampa and Green rivers in Dinosaur National Monument, listening to Al regale us with tales of Butch Cassidy and the Sundance Kid, Nik rode up beside me and smiled.

"Way to cowboy up today, Dad."

Greater praise a man could never want.

I rode that euphoric high for all of two days. The budding cowboy in me managed to stay in the saddle when Rowdy threw a fit twice. Once after a bull snuck up behind him (at about 900 bajillion miles per hour—Rowdy was napping apparently) pulling off a leaping, spinning move that even Rudolf Nureyev would have envied; and once when a rattlesnake decided to take exception to how close Rowdy was stepping to its head. I pointed out that on neither occasion were his hooves properly pointed, however, so he could just forget ballet as a career—Rowdy was not amused.

My soul and hands were baptized with blood when, after Rowdy did his job containing the herd and helping to separate out a bull calf for Al to rope, a knife was pressed into my hands and Scott motioned me down to earth. Rowdy seemed a little bit too interested, peering over my shoulder as I was shown how to squeeze the young bull's testicles down into the sack and then cleanly and surgically cut them off. If anyone asks, you do not want to eat Rocky Mountain Oysters—they have nothing whatsoever to do with seafood.

The last day we rodeoed. It was Al's idea that by finishing up the trip with three rodeo events, we would pull together all that we had learned over the week and really learn to ride rather than cling to our horses. By some miracle, Rowdy and I came in second in the flag race—an event requiring blazing speed from the horse and some deft riding skills to maneuver him around barrels while leaning over to pull a flag out of a bucket in one and then placing it in the other, all without the flag falling out of the bucket or the rider falling off the horse. Rowdy confided in me after the race that we could have won had I been wearing Wranglers, and I don't doubt it for a minute. The fact that I could understand what my horse was saying to me has no bearing on the fact that the sun was hot and the day very, very dry.

Before our group drove off into the sunset, Al presented each of us with a shiny new horseshoe nail. Polly, Al and Scott all wore one tucked into the band of their cowboy hats. It was our graduation gift and an acknowledgment that we had learned to "sweat the small stuff." Even as I write this, I hear Al reciting: "For want of a nail, a shoe was lost. For want of a shoe, a horse was lost. For want of a horse, a soldier was lost. For want of a soldier, a battle was lost. For want of a battle, my country was lost."

I still wear that horseshoe nail. It's tucked into the band on my canvas hat, the one I wear with my nylon pants, but don't tell Al 'cause it'll break his heart.

Snaggletooth:
A Portage Too Far

By Bill Cross

No mother deserved this fate—not even mine. True, my mother had done some unforgivable things to me as a child, things that inspired permanent, smoldering resentment. Like the morning in sixth grade when she flagged down my school bus as it pulled away from the stop across from my house. At first all I heard was a woman's wild screaming—probably some incoherent street person, I thought, or a neighbor whose terrier had just been flattened under our wheels. Then—to my horror—my mother marched up the front steps of the bus carrying the sack lunch I had forgotten. She held it up like a dead rat for all to see, her eyes blazing with triumph. I died a thousand deaths when I saw her wearing her pastel blue nightgown with matching slippers and hair net.

But even searing memories like these—even the burden of massive therapy bills as an adult—are a poor excuse for drowning one's mother, which is essentially what I was doing at the moment. I could see her frail form huddled in the front of the raft, ducking to keep from being decapitated by the overhanging rocks. At the same time, muddy, frigid water was rising rapidly around her as our over-loaded boat began to flood. The situation looked grim. In a moment, she would either be beheaded or drowned.

Now I swear this was all unintentional—at least, it seemed unintentional, but Freud would no doubt quibble with me on this point. This was supposed to be a family pleasure cruise down the Dolores River in southwestern Colorado, but my inexperience had turned it into a remake of *The Poseidon Adventure*. The groundwork for disaster had been laid the previous summer when I attended a white-water rafting school that gave me just enough knowledge to be dangerous. The following spring I decided to treat my family to an

61

introductory whitewater adventure—something with a little thrill, but no real risk. In those dark ages of river running, there were few guidebooks, so I based my selection on a one-paragraph description from an outfitter's catalog, which described the Dolores as an allegedly "intermediate run through spectacular desert canyons."

The canyons were indeed spectacular, but as we quickly discovered the river was not even remotely intermediate. Granted, under normal conditions most of the rapids would rate Class III, but this particular spring a record snowpack had turned the Dolores into a raging torrent of icy brown water. Our raft was just a puny speck of flotsam being swept along like a dead cow in a flash flood.

And high water was only the first strike against us.

Strike two was our paddle crew, consisting of myself, my parents and my two sisters. Five was a pretty slim number to drive our 16-foot raft. To make matters worse, two of us were not what you would call able-bodied: my father had the metabolism of a hyperactive squirrel and the physique of an anorexic; and my mother, though we told her otherwise, was a totally ineffectual paddler, in part due to her unnerving tendency to stop paddling at critical moments—just above a massive, knife-edged boulder, for example—to relate an amusing anecdote or point out an interesting bird. I tried to balance these twin parental handicaps by placing them on opposite sides of the raft, each assisted by one able-bodied sister. Meanwhile I sat in the stern calling out commands and generally promoting the myth that I knew what the hell I was doing.

Strike three was our load. Though we planned to be on the river only five days, we were carrying enough baggage, food and sundries to outfit an Everest expedition. All this paraphernalia was piled amidships in a mountainous heap, making our overburdened raft sag like a swaybacked pack horse. The combined effect of strikes one, two and three was devastating; pitting our raft and crew against the Dolores in flood was like putting a trolling motor on a battleship and sailing into a hurricane. General Custer's point spread with the Sioux was better than ours.

Finally, in a surfeit of bad luck, we faced strike four: Snaggletooth, the meanest rapid on the run. Normally a challenging Class IV, Snaggletooth was now a raging Class V gauntlet of towering waves and churning holes. Inexperienced though I was, I could see that any attempt to run Snaggletooth in our overloaded ark would be promptly and unequivocally fatal. So I opted to portage. It took us nearly half a day to lug our immense pile of gear around the rapid, and another couple of hours to relash it to the raft.

I was just finishing tying down the load when a guide from a commercial raft trip paused in his scouting of Snaggletooth and sauntered over to deliver some disturbing news. Snaggletooth, he told me, was just the beginning of our troubles. Pointing directly below where we were relaunching our raft, he related the grisly tale of Cannonball Wall: a series of violent waves and holes which led straight into a dangerously undercut rock wall on the right; anything that got sucked into the undercut would be pinned helplessly by the force of the current, squashed to jelly by tons of water pressure.

Clearly the prudent course for us now was to portage The Wall, but the first portage around Snaggletooth had cost us the better part of a day and exhausted most of my family's waning reserves of strength and patience. So, turning a deaf ear to my better judgment, I committed my own flesh and blood to a watery doom.

We shoved off. The guide had advised me to skirt the initial holes and waves so that our boat would not become swamped with water—because a swamped raft, he had confided with a snicker, wouldn't have a snowball's chance in hell.

It took us just three seconds to swamp the raft to the brim as we slammed into the first wave broadside. From then on we were history, careening downriver sideways, our world flashing wildly from murky darkness to blinding sunlight as we were alternately smothered by tons of falling water, then lofted to the peaks of massive waves. Each time I tried to shout a command, the Dolores rammed a quart of foamy brown snowmelt into my mouth. It felt like some team of sadistic nurses was giving me ice-cold enemas in every conceivable orifice at once. All the while the river kept sucking us relentlessly to the right, straight toward The Wall.

All efforts to escape our fate were in vain. My father, awash in an internal flood of adrenaline, became a paddling fiend, his blade a blur as he lashed the water in a spasm of short, jerky strokes. But it was sound and fury signifying nothing, for though he huffed and puffed like a crazed steam engine, his paddle barely touched the water and he merely whipped the top couple of inches to froth. My sisters fought a gallant but losing battle against the Dolores. And my mother, paddling in the bow, did what she usually did: she stopped paddling altogether and turned to face the rest of us, her head cocked to one side, smiling reminiscently as though she had just been reminded of a story....

Suddenly, like an elephant at full gallop, we hit The Wall. Instead of being pinned against the undercut, we were dragged along beneath it, trapped between a rushing sheet of roaring brown water

below and an angled roof of jagged red sandstone above. The strip
of air in between rapidly narrowed as our raft slid deeper into the
dark, wedge-shaped slot. The right bow—my mother's corner of the
boat—was taking the worst of it, being stuffed like a sock into that
crack of doom.

Meanwhile, pieces of gear were being stripped from the top of the
load by the rocks flashing by overhead. Our rapidly dwindling
mountain of equipment was now the only thing keeping some clear-
ance between the rocks and the river, the only thing standing
between my mother and a watery grave.

It was a ghastly sight, almost as horrible as the image of my
mother in her nightie at the front of the school bus. I was just beginning to ponder the karmic connection when, in a giant version of the
Heimlich maneuver, the full force of the Dolores River in spring
flood blasted us out the downstream end of the crack like a mangled,
half-chewed piece of sirloin forced from the windpipe of a choking
person. In a flash of blessed sunshine, we burst free! But lo, we had
been changed mightily; our raft, which only seconds before had been
the picture of family fun, now emerged from Cannonball Wall as the
Ghost Ship of the Dolores, trailing shards of gear and streamers of
frayed rope.

We exchanged wide-eyed, ashen-faced looks—all except my
father, who was still puffing and paddling like a madman. I surveyed
the damage. Our vast mound of gear had been pruned a bit, but what
the hell, we had plenty to spare. The important thing was we were
alive and, aside from a few scrapes, unhurt.

My mother frowned at me over her sunglasses in a quizzical,
slightly suspicious way. "I assume that was unintentional?" she
asked.

"Hell yes!" I replied emphatically.

And that's the truth. It really was an accident, no matter what
Freud might say. You think I'd try to drown my own mother? Just
because she scarred me for life by parading around in front of my
sixth-grade class in her nightgown? Listen, buddy, sometimes a cigar
is just a cigar. I may be neurotic, but I'm not crazy.

The Legend of
Waterdog Jack

By Michael Shepherd

Big Muskie was a fat, 6-foot muskellunge that few believed existed. Too damned big, people said. Muskies aren't indigenous to Northern California's Lake Chabot and, though a few had been covertly planted there, they weren't known to get that big anywhere. Big Muskie did exist. As did a few other unusual, non-indigenous critters that had moved in. One of which, did not like company.

The first time I saw the object of my obsession, I was hiding on a scrub-patched hill overlooking Bass Cove. Off limits. Again. I was 16 that spring of '75. And on a mission. I had been scrutinizing the shallows through my binoculars when seven macaques, descendants of pardoned escapees from nearby Knowland Park Zoo, slipped from the forest for a drink. Macaques were publicly accepted, and welcome facet of Chabot, and I watched with intrigue as an adolescent waded-in and playfully splashed about.

Bummer for that one. Big Muskie exploded from the depths and caught the horrified monkey in midleap. The dark-green monster thrashed, broke tulies and chomped for a better grip. Then dragged its frenzied victim into the depths, severing the macaque's screams like a guillotine. The victim's freaked-out kin scattered, howling into the forest. Startled great blue herons, quail and flocks of other squawking birds erupted form the hills and trees. Adrenaline zapped my whole body and the pit of my gut loosed a wholehearted, "Holy shit!"

Big Muskie was as big as they'd said—and some. Right then, I swore to all the fishing gods that I'd catch that giant. And, at last, I knew what I needed. Big. Fat. Live. Bait.

Fairmont Drive ascends eastward out of San Leandro's suburban sprawl and winds over the first range of the East Bay hills. Sparse eucalyptus and grassy hills etched with scrub-choked ravines greet approaching lakegoers, belying the beckoning beauty of the bluish-green lake and its 12 miles of thickly forested backcountry. A

beautifully set jewel that suddenly appears to the left as Fairmont swoops down to Lake Chabot's entrance and south end.

Lake Chabot is a meandering, Y-shaped reservoir, rimmed with eucalyptus, oak and deciduous trees. Redwood, pine and fir dominate the backcountry. Mountain lion and bobcat hunt black-tailed deer, possum and 'coon. The skunks do what they please.

Chabot's right fork snakes eastward. The left fork goes northward over a mile, then bottlenecks to just a hundred yards across. Beyond the bottleneck, the lake opens to a perpendicular, yam-shaped bay. The fat, west end of the bay curves left a quarter mile to the 115-foot dam. The bay tapers northward a half mile, then spreads into three long fingers. One points north, and two point east. Bass Cove is the entrance to these backwaters. The area is actually wrinkled with many wooded coves.

Great fishing there, but Bass Cove and its backcountry was off limits to the public in those days.

Yeah, right. Bass Cove was Big Muskie's territory. Me and Eddie weren't about to let that shiny-shoed, starch can of a nitpicking ranger, Ricky Butz, keep us out of there.

Carrot-topped Eddie Dawkins was my pard. Short, stocky and cockstrong, Eddie was game for anything. His light-green eyes had glittered when I told him about Big Muskie's awesome debut. For the next few months, he rode with me on every foray into Bass Cove.

Bass Cove was easy to hide in, but Butz would switch to his electric motor, hug the tulies and get us like that. He patrolled often and had caught us back there several times. Once, he tossed our poles into the lake, put us into his boat and ranted about mountain lions, off-limits, blah, blah, all the way to the south end. Another time, he took us to Juvenile Hall, where we sat for hours till our parents came. That time, we had to return for court. The judge had said, "Next time, it's 90 days in Boy's Ranch." Bang.

Butz was overdoing it. I mean, what was the big deal about Bass Cove? He was the only ranger assigned to patrol Chabot, and he couldn't be over 22. Hell, seemed like everything he did shouted, "Hey, I'm King Shit!" I just figured the jerk believed that.

Then I learned about Waterdog Jack.

Me and Eddie were on the marina dock munching nuked burritos for breakfast and plotting our route to Bass Cove, when Butz's boat pulled into the marina and docked. Eddie pulled his beanie lower and I flipped-on my sweatshirt hood. We eased behind a trash bin and sat on the wooden bench. Nonchalantly, we peeked around the bin.

Butz looked rattled. He barked at the dock boy and stumbled out of the boat. His right foot slipped off the dock into the water, up to his hip. That sure puckered his butt 'cause he was up quick, jitter-dancing and cussing the scrawny ol' buck-toothed dock boy. We laughed...then stopped.

The dock boy was swaying and gawking at a big lump inside the boat. He promptly barfed into the water, feeding the bluegills under the dock.

Butz and a man in an orange vest finally wobbled onto the boat and began unloading the big lump: a bloated corpse. Whoa. We walked over and blended with the onlookers. Whew. Looked like crawdads and things had scarfed on it some. Damned thing might have once been someone's grandpa, but not any more. It didn't even look real. It had a rubbery, open-mouthed, cartoon-like face...and looked a mite surprised at being dead. Me and Eddie stood green-gilled and bug-eyed while they wrestled the smelly thing out of the boat. Butz's face scrunched-up so tight that his little blond mustache disappeared under his nose, and I thought he too might feed the bluegills any second. He never even noticed us.

The body stunk bad, and gagged everyone back. "Looks like another drunk fisherman drowned," someone said. "Been happening a lot the last couple years."

"He drowned all right," a knobby old black man mumbled to himself. "Waterdog Jack don't like trespassers fishin' his end of the lake."

Waterdog Jack? I had fished all around Lake Chabot since it had opened to the public in '69. And I had never heard of Waterdog Jack. Me and Eddie looked at each other, at the corpse Butz was covering, then at the old man lumbering toward the road with his pole and white bucket of catfish. "Hey mister!" we yelled, running after him. "Whaddaya mean? Who's Waterdog Jack?"

The man ignored us. He reached the road and kept walking toward the parking lot. We flanked and pestered him till he stopped. He looked around. No one was near. He set down his bucket. His thin face hardened and he said: "You're them boys Butz is always catching in Bass Cove. Well, you best stay out of there, ya hear?"

"What about Waterdog Jack?" I repeated. "Who's he?"

"Aw, dog it," he said. "I guess y'all better know about Waterdog Jack...," his face jutted at us, "...before he gets you!

"Follow the West Shore Road to the end," he said. "Go over the do not enter gate and follow the road till it forks down to the lake. The maintenance man, Theobald Flynn, lives down there. I just left him. Tell him Country sent you. Ask him about Waterdog Jack.

Theobald thinks he's harmless. But he ain't. Remember that boys. He ain't. And dog it, stay clear o' that water back there!" Country took his bucket and left.

We had a mystery—dead body and all! We fetched our 10-speeds, made sure our bait cages were secure and pedaled off like our butts were on fire.

The late-morning sun was well into its daylong roast when we reached the gate. A pair of low-flying vultures glided by on the hunt. Insects buzzed in the blackberry thickets. I was hot and sweaty and I shucked out of my sweatshirt. I stuffed it beside my bait box and the bait scrabbled around in there. Poor critter was going to shit when showtime came.

We lifted our bikes over and headed out. The forest thickened ahead and canopied the dirt road, forming a long, sunless tunnel. The temperature dropped about 20 degrees when we rode into it. The breeze rippled my sweaty T-shirt and chilled me. A raven cawed somewhere up the mountain to our left.

We knew where the maintenance man's spot was, but we'd always steered clear. We'd seen him around, putting up signs, planting trees and such. He pretty much avoided folks and minded his own business. With all those prison tattoos on his arms, I'm sure folks were of a like mind and left him alone, too. We sure had. Until now.

At last, the fork appeared. We followed the right fork down, riding our brakes to keep our speed down. The trees thinned and the lake appeared. Sunlight broke through in patches. Cool shade and hot sunlight flickered on my skin as the road veered down to the right. A hundred yards from the fork above, the road ended at a small clearing rimmed with redwoods.

Tulies lined the lake, now to our left, except for a 5-yard stretch. An aluminum canoe was beached half out of the water. Twenty yards up the bank, a silver Airstream with a canvas awning faced the lake. A powerline strung down the mountain to a pole next to the trailer. A redwood picnic bench with an ice chest beside it, rounded out the site.

"Mr. Flynn?" I called out. "Hey, Mr. Flynn, you home?" No answer. We parked our bikes and I knocked on the door while Eddie poked around. "I guess he ain't here," I concluded.

Eddie popped open a can of Coors he'd fished from the ice chest and took a long guzzle.

"What are you doing, fool?" I scolded, scanning the area again for Mr. Flynn.

"Aw, don't sweat it, Mike," he said, and burped. "Come on, let's go. There's no such thing as a Waterdog Jack creeping around these hills killing people. If there was, search teams'd be everywhere. And we'd've heard. That ol' man, Country, is full of shit. And so's Thee-oh-BALD Flynn if he's blabbering that same crap. C'mon, let's go catch..."

"There is 'such thing as a Waterdog Jack," a cavernous voice announced. "But he doesn't kill people, and he doesn't creep around these hills." Theobald Flynn stepped from the forest, and added, "Waterdog Jack lives in the lake."

Dark, raw-boned and hatchet-faced, his strong 50-year-old grin and amused blue eyes dared us to disbelieve him. "Thee-oh-BALD Flynn, at your service," he said, looking directly at Eddie, who was a good foot shorter, shrinking the boy even more with his grin.

"Aw, hey...I, uh..." Eddie fumbled, ineffectively concealing the Coors can.

"Country told you about Waterdog Jack, huh?" Theobald Flynn turned—to Eddie's relief—and asked me, tipping back his black cowboy hat. He wore jeans, brown hiking boots and a black T-shirt. Nothing softened the impact of all those tattoos of Vikings, dragons and women sleeving his arms.

"Yes, sir," I said. "Butz pulled a body from the lake, and Country said Waterdog Jack didn't like people fishing his end of the lake. He said we should ask you about Waterdog Jack. Oh, I'm Mike, and this is Eddie, Mr. Flynn."

"Call me Theobald, fellas," he said, walking to the ice chest. "Pretty hot today, Mike. Orange Crush or beer?"

"Beer," I said, surprised at the offer. "Thanks."

"What do you mean, Waterdog Jack lives in the lake?" Eddie asked. "How does he breathe?" He added with a skeptical edge, his courage seeping back.

"Well, he's not some fish-man. He breathes air like everyone else. He's an oddball, though. No doubt about that."

"Does Butz know about him?" I asked.

"Yup. And he almost lost his job trying to explain to his superiors that he believed a man living in the lake was drowning people. Butz, Country and a few regulars think Waterdog Jack is yanking folks right out of their boats. Ha! That's all hooey. Those drownings were accidents. Period. Waterdog Jack is just a harmless ol' weirdo, that's all." He patted the tabletop and said, "Let's have a seat, and I'll tell you about Waterdog Jack."

We climbed up and sat in the sun, facing the lake. Theobald sat on my right, Eddie on my left. I could see Bass Cove a half mile across the bay.

"The world is full of oddballs," he began. "We just don't see a lot of them. I've seen some live ones in my day, though. Many of them end up in prison—"

"What were you in prison for?" Eddie interrupted.

"When I wasn't much older than you, I killed a man, over a woman. I did 20 years," he said, pensively.

Eddie took a sip and hushed.

"Anyhow," Theobald continued. "You got hobos living in abandoned subway tunnels under New York City, some who don't surface for years. Hermits that seek solitude in nooks and crannies all around the world...Waterdog Jack is like that.

"Waterdog Jack Finney was the star of the Arroyo High swim team in the mid-60s. A 6-foot 4-inch bonerack that could swim like the dickens. He wet to 'Nam in '66 and got captured near the end of his tour. He eventually escaped, and came home all screwed-up. People bothered him too much, so he came here, to his boyhood playground. To stay."

"But Chabot didn't open to the public till '69," I said.

"Exactly," he said.

"That still doesn't explain how he could live underwater," Eddie pointed out, covertly elbowing me.

"This story began a hundred years ago, Eddie. I'll start there. In 1874, Anthony Chabot built this reservoir for the East Bay settlements. He employed 800 Chinese laborers to remove the rocks and soil from this valley. He used 200 wild horses to tramp a mixture of silt and clay in layers to form the lake bottom. While removing the rocks, the Chinese found a cave entrance 40 feet below the intended water line. A hidden hole, just big enough for a man to fit through. The Tong leaders ordered the Chinese to keep the cave secret from Chabot and his white overseers. They found a labyrinth beneath those hills," Theobald nodded toward Bass Cove, "filled with Indian artifacts, skeletons and gold.

"In 1875, the reservoir was filled, and declared off-limits to the public. In 1925, my Uncle Sam heard the story from Wu, his family's old Chinese cook. In 1928, a long drought had dropped the lake's level by two-thirds. Sam found the cave's entrance right where Wu said it would be. He found that the Chinese had taken everything decades earlier. The lake was refilled and has remained so ever since.

"Sam told this story to his grandson, Jack Finney," Theobald paused, an almost imperceptible expression resembling pity, passed over his face, then said, "Waterdog Jack is my second cousin."

"Oh...," I said.

"So he lives in the cave, not in the lake!" Eddie blurted, elbowing me again. "But he hast to swim to get in, or out, right?"

"Right," Theobald said. "As crazy as he is, he's figured out how to farm oxygen from the vegetation down there. He has oxygen pockets rigged all across the bottom. He swims out, checks his fish traps, and never has to surface. He just pokes his head up to an air pocket for a few breaths, and swims on. The vegetation beneath replenishes the oxygen. That's why hardly anyone believes he exists. He rarely comes up. He just wants solitude...hell some hermits choose mountain tops, ol' Jack chose a lake bottom instead. That doesn't make him a killer."

After we told Theobald about our hunt for Big Muskie, we wrapped up our visit. Just before we pedaled-off, he took Eddie's arm and said: "Eddie, slow down while you're still young. The cemeteries and prisons are full of smart asses like you. Believe that, son. Slow down."

Eddie looked at him blankly, and said, "Sure, thanks, Mr. Flynn."

Once we got out of earshot, Eddie sneered: "That guy's crazier than a Berzerkeley hippie at a la-dee-da concert! You don't believe all that shit, do ya...?!"

I wasn't really sure if I did, but I said, "Nah."

Back on the road, we continued around till we reached Bass Cove. We got our gear together and stashed our bikes. We climbed down through 50 yards of forest, grabbing brush and exposed roots to keep from slipping. At the bottom, the water looked clear and deep. The opposite shore was about 50 yards away.

"I'll take that wide spot toward the back," I said. I needed room for my dad's 9-foot pole.

"OK," Eddie said. "I'll take that patch of beach up this way."

"Good luck, bud!" I said.

"Good luck!" He replied.

We reached our respective spots and started rigging-up. I was putting on my leather gloves for handling the bait, when Eddie yelled: "Hold on, Mike. Let's cast at the same time, OK? But I gotta shit first. I don't want to be fighting Big Muskie while I gotta shit!"

"Aw, man," I groaned. "Hurry up! Let me know when you're done!" Jeez...

That Eddie. Hunkered down, Levi's bunched around his black logger's boots, pale, Irish butt glowing in the sunlight, taking a damned grunt.

Right on cue, from Eddie's side, Butz's boat slid around the bend.

I was back some and had a chance. I scrambled-up into thick brush and hid. My heart pounded like a kettle drum as I watched.

Eddie duck-walked closer to the tulies and scooched-in close, but that was a sight Butz couldn't miss if he wanted to.

"Hold it right there, Mr. Dawkins!" Butz shouted. "Don't MOVE! I just pulled a body form here, you idiot! Where's your friend? I told you boys it was dangerous back here, damn it!" He hopped to shore and stood, fists on his hips, just 10 feet from Eddie. "Hurry it up, Dawkins!" he barked.

Embarrassment reddened Eddie's face as Butz's authoritative eyes watched him finish his business. Boy, Butz was a cold dude.

Butz cuffed Eddie and loaded him, his bait and his gear onto the boat. Boy's Ranch. Ninety days for Eddie. And he knew it.

Butz started his Mercury and cruised around looking for me. Looked right at me once and my pounding heart tried hard to betray me. He gunned it around and they were gone. Whew...he didn't see me. The motor's drone soon faded into the distance.

It sure was quiet. I crawled from the bushes, dusted myself off and looked around. Even with the sun out, the forest sure had a lot of dark places. And the water sure looked deep. Butz had said he'd pulled that body from right here somewhere. Country had said Waterdog Jack was not harmless...

The bait scrabbled around in its cage and I snapped out of it. I had a monster fish to catch! At long last, my bait would finally get wet. I had trapped two of them after I saw Big Muskie, and for three months, I let them live a glutton's dream. Tempted, and pestered by Eddie so many times to bring them prematurely, I stuck to my original plan and let them fatten to an obese, 15 pounds each.

I got my setup ready: a homemade leather and Styrofoam floatation vest for the bait, rigged with a foot-long shank to go under its belly from head to pooper, and a big, 03 treble hook on the end. OK. I pulled-out the combative, black sewer rat and wrestled the pissed-off critter into its vest and got it cinched-up. I walked to an open stretch of bank and popped the shank's eyelet onto my line's giant snapswivel. That ol' wiggling, cat-sized rat put a good bend in my pole when I hefted it up. Okie-dokie. I eased my whole body into a rotating, one-and-a-half swing and let that booger fly...

...SLAP. Right out into the middle. It swam every which way and I got juiced watching it. If Big Muskie was around, there was no way he'd pass on this meal.

The rat swam toward the far side, and I let it get near there before pulling it back to the middle. It eventually tired and the vest kept it from drowning. After a short rest, I nudged it and it started swimming toward my side. I reeled-in the slack and focused on the rat, willing Big Muskie to burst from the depths and swallow it whole.

Then...

Choop! That booger got sucked under—hard. I yanked back, once, twice, three times! YEAH!

Nope. A few seconds into the fight, I knew it wasn't Big Muskie. Damn. Had to be a largemouth bass. Fifteen, maybe 20 pounds. A record at Chabot for sure, but I wasn't here for that. Damned thing mangled my bait for Big Muskie. No way it could swallow that big ol' rat. I fought that ol' bass anyway, but I swore that sucker was getting scaled, gutted and fried, for messing up my bait.

Movement to my left. Something disturbed the water on the deep side of the tulies. A long shadow swam past, toward the bass. Big Muskie...?

Waterdog Jack...?

My gizzard froze. Goosebumps raced across my skin...

WHAM! I yanked, once, twice, three times! I fell on my butt and slid into the water to my waist. Yow! My shoulder blades clawed dirt and pulled me up from Waterdog Jack's domain. I flipped the line release and scrambled well onto the bank. I flipped back the release, reeled-in all the slack, fixed the drag and it-was-ON!

That bad-assed Muskie was strong! Zinging line off my reel like it was nothing. He headed-out to deeper water and I sloshed along the bank holding my pole high so the line cleared the tulies. After 50 yards, the bay widened and I reached an open stretch of shore. I parked it right there and stomped my boot heels into soft earth. Yessiree, talking about a battle!

A half-hour later, my whole body ached and I still hadn't gotten a look at Big Muskie. I was out in the open and I half expected Butz to return any time. I kept an eye out.

Big Muskie weakened, and 15 minutes later, I saw him. He looked a bit like a legless alligator. A few minutes more and a few yards closer...he thrashed with renewed strength, just 5 yards out. Boy, what a monster! An easy 6-footer. Easy. And fat, like he'd been eating two monkeys a day since the first time I saw him!

I was thinking, how in the hell am I going to get this thing home, when I saw Theobald Flynn at the far end of the bay, rowing over in his canoe. He must have seen me through his binoculars fighting Big Muskie, I figured.

I got Big Muskie near the shore and I stepped-in to get a hand inside his gill slit. He was done, I put my weight into pulling him onto the shore, then twisted out the hook. All that was left of that rat was its head, mangled forelegs, and a few things stringing from its chest cavity. A big piece of bass lip remained on one of the hooks. What a day! What a monster fish!

My day wasn't over just yet...

Like a dolphin, that naked, stringy-haired lunatic leapt from the lake and landed right on top of me. Stark, shitless terror practically blew all my guts inside out. I hollered my head off and fought maniacally. He was cold and clammy and rank like he'd been dead a week. He grappled and gripped with green-nailed hands, and I kicked and punched and my heart was banging right out of my chest. His twisted face and bloodshot eyes—he was NUTS! Growling, dragging me...the lake enveloped my legs! Oh no, not me, Jack. I popped him a couple good ones in the face and I scrambled back up the bank. He scurried after me. He was ghastly pale and covered with big red sores. And leeches. He grabbed my legs and pulled with the strength that only lunatics can muster. I was in the lake again. Thrashing. I swallowed water and coughed it back out through my nose. I tasted my own salty snot and I knew I'd be dead in moments...

"HEY, HEY, HEY!" Theobald bellowed. "Let him go, Finney! Let him go, damn it!"

Theobald leapt ashore carrying a big knife. Waterdog Jack looked up and froze. I kicked him dead on his nose. And broke it. He howled and I scrambled clear. We all stood, looking wildly at one another...

Waterdog Jack ignored his blood-streaming nose and glowered at his second cousin. Theobald looked back, shaking his head in what looked like pained, disbelief. Waterdog Jack glanced at me briefly, glared at Theobald once more, then took a long, arcing dive and disappeared into the lake.

Except for my own labored breathing, Bass Cove was silent for nearly a minute. I was shaken right down to my soggy boots, but quite relieved.

"I just refused to believe it," Theobald said, finally. "Mike, I'm sorry. I just didn't believe that he'd ever hurt a soul. Are you OK?"

"Yeah," I said, inspecting my mud-caked body, "scared the living shit out of me, but I'm OK."

Big Muskie had slipped back into the lake during the ruckus. Well, I figured, I'm alive, and I got a hell of a fight out of the deal. Two of 'em. I thanked Theobald for coming to the rescue, but declined his offer to take me across in his canoe. The mountains had cast long shadows across the lake by then, and I just wanted to go. I labored back up the hillside, got both bikes and left. I was done with Lake Chabot.

A month later, a small article in the newspaper reported that the body of Lake Chabot's maintenance man, Theobald Gregory Flynn, had been pulled from the lake. An accidental drowning it said.

Right.

It took me 15 years to return to Lake Chabot. From time to time, I had "seen" Waterdog Jack in the shadows, outside my windows on rainy nights and in my nightmares. I had to return and bury my fears once and for all. Hell, I was a grown man, and I had no business harboring such fear over some nutcase. For a kid, I had done OK anyhow, I broke that bastard's nose after all, didn't I?

So there I was, 15 years later, fishing a half mile up the West Shore Road when Butz pulled up in his truck. He remembered me and came down to say hi. His mustache had filled-out and he had some gray around his ears. Hiking boots had replaced those old shiny shoes, and he seemed much more relaxed. It was a June morning. A weekday. And we were alone on the shore.

"Any luck?" he asked.

"A couple rainbow so far," I said, eyeing him. He looked tough. And mellowed. "Seen him lately?" I asked.

He didn't answer right away. He hunkered down beside me, picked up a few pebbles and rattled them lightly in his fist. "About four years back," he said, "we found another fisherman floating in the tulies east of the dam. Drowned. It was ruled an accident, like the others. I saw Waterdog Jack some weeks later and shot at him. He was out of range, though, and once he hits that water, well, he's gone. I know I missed him." He tossed a pebble into the water and we watched it sink. A 5-inch largemouth rushed-up to investigate. "I haven't seen him since," he added. "And there's been no more drownings."

I tightened my line with a turn of my old Garcia 300's handle, and asked, "Still can't prove he exists?"

"Nope." Butz tossed in another pebble. The little bass attacked it, sucked it in and spit it out, pissed. "I think he moved on, migrated to another lake, or a river.... I made it too hot for him here. You know, I dragged Bass Cove and pulled-up a bunch of 5-gallon buckets? He had 'em rigged-up to hold oxygen. Yup, even his twisted mind must have sensed that it was just a matter of time. I know this though, Waterdog Jack is one sick puppy. Whatever territory he stakes out for himself, he'll drown any loners he catches in it. He'll drag 'em into the depths like all the others."

I nodded, knowing the full-well, "Clearlake, Berryessa, Comanche," I said. "Hell, in four years, he could be anywhere."

He tossed in his last pebble. The bass rushed it, and stopped short, aggressively fanning its pectoral fins. Butz said, "Yup."

Horseplay

By Ronald Bourret

The first thing you need to understand about horses is that they are not big dogs. They don't wag their tails or lick your face, they don't chase balls or fetch the newspaper, and they most certainly don't roll on their back and beg for you to scratch their belly. Of this latter trait—or lack thereof—I am heartily glad, for if they involuntarily twitched their hind leg like a dog does when you scratch their belly, the resulting kick would probably buy a second Porsche for your local plastic surgeon.

About the only thing horses have in common with dogs is flatulence. In this respect, horses are first cousins to bulldogs, albeit on a much grander scale. And unlike dogs, horses courteously lift their tail while degassing. Although I suppose their intention is to give you a better view, it is not a pleasant sight. This undoubtedly pleases them. A hound is flatulent in the sincere hope it is improving your air quality; a horse is flatulent only as an alternative to biting you.

This leads us to the second—and more important—thing you need to understand about horses: They are ornery. In spite of this orneriness, it is possible to have a relationship with them. This is not to say that that relationship will be enjoyable. It is also possible to have a relationship with a weasel, a hyena or Leona Helmsley, but like a relationship with a horse it is not likely to be pleasant.

By now, you have probably guessed that horses do not occupy the complimentary strata of my opinions. Like cats, I cannot tell if they are stubborn or just plain stupid. At the risk of angering the cat- and horse-loving populations of the Western world, I propose that both are stupid, both are mean and neither is a dog of a different color. I will even go so far as to venture that *Black Beauty* and other movies of that ilk comprise a grand conspiracy hatched by the entertainment industry and the Horse Chow Division of the Ralston-Purina Co. The entire scheme is foisted upon innocent young girls to convince them to buy cloyingly cute plastic horses by the gross and horse chow by the dump truck full.

All of this explains Karin. As a young girl, Karin saw all the girl-loves-horse movies—including *Black Beauty*—and read all the girl-loves-horse books. She had horse dolls, horse pictures and horse clothes. Had she also learned to make hors d'oeuvres, this might have been worthwhile, but instead she acquired a horse. She also acquired a paper route to pay the Ralston-Purina Co.

You'll notice that these facts most convincingly support my theory. But Karin also claims that when she felt low, she retreated to the stable to lie next to her horse, where a subtle communion between mare and maid would raise her spirits. Why it didn't kick her through the stable wall, I'm not sure? I'm willing to suggest that the entire story is an elaborate fabrication and that she was bought off for an autographed picture of Elizabeth Taylor, a lifetime pass to *Black Beauty* and a hundredweight of horse chow.

I therefore agreed to go horseback riding with certain reservations. However, Karin had gamely gone climbing and caving with me, so it only seemed fair that I bruise both butt and ego for her. I had been riding once, about 10 years before, on a horse named Big Red. Big Red was big, about the size of a Volkswagen. He was also ornery, but I suppose that goes without saying. The girl who ran the stable told me that Red preferred eating to walking and that, if I didn't want to spend my entire ride sitting in a pasture on a browsing horse, I would need to pull his head up continually.

Big Red walked and I pulled. Halfway through the ride, my arms felt like they'd been slinging horse manure all morning, and Red was glaring at me over his shoulder. Three-quarters of the way through, he tried to peel me off his back with a tree branch. Shortly before we reached the stable, he looked one last time across his shoulder and glared hard, then broke into a dead run. Big Red was going to eat. We never spoke again.

For our first ride, Karin and I went to a trail riding stable. On a trail ride, a bunch of tourists are hoisted onto placid horses and a guide, usually a college kid or a rancher in need of a few extra bucks, leads them at a slow walk over a well-worn trail. The horses are conditioned to follow the...um...tail of the horse in front of them. To take a trail ride, you need the skill of a sack of potatoes.

This is something I can do. My job consists of sitting essentially motionless behind a desk all day long and, because they keep giving me raises, I suspect I am pretty good at it. But I was no match for my fellow tourists. These were the people elevator load limits were devised for—one family of four must have weighed in at almost half a ton—and watching them saddle up was a painful experience. When a friendly shove failed to land them on their mounts, the wranglers led both horse and payload to a picnic table where the rider fell from table to saddle. How they resisted the temptation to use a crane, I do not know.

As a sack of potatoes, I was at least self-loading. I swaggered up to my horse and swung up, worried mostly about overshooting and landing face first in a pile of horse manure on the other side. Fortunately, I avoided any such embarrassment, only to discover that my swagger had convinced the wranglers to load me onto a "spirited" horse. As I had been hoping for a "plow" horse, this was startling news.

The woman who ran the stable explained to me that Cheyenne was an old cow pony, 28 years old, and relegated to spending his days hauling about potatoes. The only thing I needed to know was that he was trained to gallop when squeezed with both thighs. She had thought him too old to gallop, but the week before a tourist had accidentally given him *the* squeeze and he had taken off like a thoroughbred on the final straight at the Preakness. I hoped a mosquito wouldn't bite me in the wrong place.

In deference to Karin's riding ability, the stable owner gave her a spunky horse and allowed her to ride last, where she could lag behind and then trot up to the group. In deference to my marital status, I was allowed to ride next to last, where I could enjoy the dust and flatulence of an entire string of horses. I had no intention of lagging and trotting, as this vastly exceeded my skill as a sack of potatoes.

We sauntered off. Karin lagged behind with a huge grin on her face. My horse—not in the least under my control—kept close to the tail of the next horse. The ride was mostly like that. I'd look ahead and see a string of embarrassed, ornery horses bowed under their colorless, obese cargo. Then I'd look back and see Karin, looking like she was born on a horse and dancing circles around our tracks.

Halfway through the ride, Karin insisted that I take her picture. Although this threatened to shatter my confidence—immensely swollen because I hadn't yet fallen off—I rose to the challenge. With a masterly display of horsemanship that Karin entirely failed to notice, I convinced Cheyenne to stop so Karin could hand me the camera. As an encore, I convinced Cheyenne to walk forward and stop again. Again, Karin seemed immune to my skill.

Confident now of my equestrian ability, I turned to take Karin's picture. Big mistake. As I lifted the camera, I also lifted the reins and unknowingly commanded Cheyenne to turn left, stop, turn right, back up, dance the Charleston, and sign up for a correspondence course in Lithuanian history. Somewhere in this confusion, I managed to snap a few pictures. I'm proud to note that not only is Karin in these pictures, but so is her horse. That both are out of focus and on the verge of laughing hysterically is irrelevant. At least, they noticed my horsemanship.

Karin left me alone after this, presumably because it hurt her stomach too much to laugh that hard. I returned to my station in the dust and flatulence, and Karin trotted merrily across field and forest. At the stables, I cautiously dismounted. I had gotten this far without being bucked or drop-kicked and was not about to give Cheyenne—still sore about having to take Lithuanian history—any chances. I tipped the woman who ran the operation $5. It seemed small recompense for the pain she must suffer trying to stifle her guffaws.

Karin was jubilant. I asked if she wanted to go again, but she said no. Twelve dollars an hour was too steep for dancing at the end of a pack train. What she really wanted was to rent a horse and just go riding. Unfortunately, the insurance industry, the personal injury lawyers and a bunch of people with as much sense of personal responsibility as a radish had conspired to make this impossible.

Nobody rented horses because no company would insure them. Renting horses had therefore become the business equivalent of withdrawing your lifesavings, converting it into quarters, and challenging the first hyperactive 8-year-old you met to a video game contest. You'd be cleaned out in no time. Consequently, most outfitters either retired or went into freight hauling, although some clever marketing people managed to rename the latter activity "trail rides."

A week later, I heard of a horse rental operation. Sure that it was some sort of scam to part gullible tourists like me from their money, I called them and asked if they "just rented horses." "Rafts, too," the voice on the phone replied. It was clear they hadn't understood my question. I pressed on, convinced there was a catch, but nothing I asked changed their mind. They were sure they rented horses. I stopped asking questions.

We arrived mid-morning to discover that all the horses were out. Karin disappeared into their little shack to fill out the liability forms. She reappeared a few minutes later to ask if I was a novice or intermediate. After a short discussion we agreed that, in spite of my extensive experience on Big Red and my masterly display of horsemanship on Cheyenne, I was a novice. They didn't have anything lower on the scale.

To pass the time, we asked the wrangler about the insurance angle. How had they found a company to insure them? Simple, he replied. They didn't have any insurance. If somebody sued them, they would just give them the whole operation: 25 horses, a corral and a few bales of hay. I must admit that I enjoyed the image of some greedy slimeball—his life ruined because a broken thumb made it impossible to channel surf—being stuck for all eternity with 25 hungry, ornery beasts.

When the horses returned, I drew another big red horse, this one named Flint. Why all the John Wayne names? I wondered. Couldn't they name any horses Bob or Irving or Matilda? On the off chance that cowboys gave their horses real cowboy names because they liked them and not just to please tourists, I decided to keep my mouth shut. I could just imagine Karin talking about our honeymoon years later.

"...and when we finally found a place that actually rented horses, Ron just had to ask if they had one named Irving. The wrangler not only refused to rent to us, he threatened to kick our citified asses clear across the county if we weren't gone in two minutes."

Instead, I stood next to the corral with my hands in my pockets, trying not to look too incompetent and moving occasionally to avoid the business (rear) end of Flint. I had heard somewhere that they kicked, too. While waiting, I listened to a spirited discussion between the wrangler and the previous rider about Flint's right front leg. Apparently, it was still recovering from an injury and Flint stumbled on it occasionally.

Oh, great, I thought. First, they're going to load me on this ornery brute, then his leg's going to fall off and he's going to land on me. There I'll be, a little pile of people goo with broken thumbs and not a chance of ever changing channels again in my life and probably stuck forever on the Home Shopping Network. A bunch of personal injury lawyers will surround me and try to convince me to sue for ownership of 25 defective horses. Karin must hate me to take me to stables like this.

Five minutes later, I had other things to worry about. I had mounted Flint and discovered that, like Big Red and Cheyenne, he had no interest in hauling me anywhere. Karin's horse, Rocky, was of a similar mind, but Karin patiently explained to him why he was mistaken. While Rocky listened to Karin and gave little horsey-yes, uh-huh, I-see-your-point shakes of his head, Flint headed for the hay. All I can figure is that horses have a Sack-O-Potatoes Meter hidden under their saddle blanket and, while Karin didn't even register, I weighed in at Buckets O' Russets.

Through it all, the wrangler kept a straight face. He patiently led Flint away from the corral and, every 5 feet or so, gave me the reins. I would kick Flint with my heels, shout "Giddap" or click my teeth—both of which I had been convinced since the age of 4 were the magic words that made all horses go—and then just sit there. The view was pleasant, but it hardly compensated for the wholesale destruction of my childhood illusions. Flint would lean down, tear off a mouthful of grass and look back at me as if to say this wasn't his childhood dream either. Then he would turn and start back toward the hay bar. The wrangler would retrieve the reins, drag Flint another 5 feet and start the process over.

When we were about 50 feet from the corral, the wrangler picked up a stick, gave it to me, telling me to use it as a riding crop. Not wanting to hurt Flint, I tickled his hindquarter with it. "Harder," said the wrangler. I slapped lightly. "*Hit him*," said the wrangler. Here I was, sitting on a beast the size of a Toyota and I was worried about hurting him with a small stick. I looked quickly around to make sure there were no representatives of PAWS in the immediate vicinity and let him have it. He strolled off. What do they use to make these things gallop? I wondered. A two-by-four?

The trail followed a fence line that paralleled the highway for about a quarter mile, then turned onto a dirt road that wound past some fields and into the hills. We had walked a few hundred feet when we met a party of riders coming the other way. The horses greeted each other with a few snorts, which I assume meant something like this:

"Headin' in?"

"Yep. You?"

"Out."

"Still see ya got one o' them damn tourists on yer back."

"Yep. Been thinkin' about buckin' him off."

"Tried that once. No oats for a week."

"Oats? Did you say oats?"

At this point, Flint wheeled to the right and started to follow the other horses back to the corral. Karin's horse stood placidly by, chewing a mouthful of grass and providing Karin a magnificent platform from which to view my troubles. It seemed that Karin had entered into some sort of subtle communion with him which, while not necessarily an agreement to follow her instructions, was at least an agreement to make me look bad. Horses are ornery, or hadn't I mentioned that?

I pulled on Flint's left rein, somebody having told me that this was the way to make a horse turn left. He turned a few degrees and stopped. I pulled harder. Nothing. Karin tactfully—I think her comment began with, "Hey, moron..." pointed out that I was also pulling back on the rein. This was the command to back up and explained why Flint had gotten close enough to the highway to stick out his hoof and attempt to hitch back to the corral.

I stopped pulling back on the reins and just pulled left. Flint turned right toward the corral. I gave up on the left turn altogether and pulled on the right rein, hoping to turn Flint all the way around until we were facing left. It worked. Not only had I been given a horse with a faulty right front tire, it also had a broken steering wheel.

We turned (right) from the trail onto the road. I noticed that after a short distance, the road veered to the right of a fence and into some barns. To the left of the fence was the road we wanted. Panic stricken, I realized I would have to guide Flint around some mud puddles between the two roads, doing it in the next 50 feet or risk being stuck on the wrong side of the fence. I imagined the owner of the barns talking to his wife:

"Hey, Mabel, come look at this. Some city slicker sitting on a horse out next to the fence."

"Well, why's he jest sittin' there? Why doesn't he ride around the fence? Thet's sartainly a pretty girl on the other side o' the fence, and if I were a city slicker, I'd want ta be over thar with her."

"I dunno, Mabel. From the looks of it, they gave him thet horse with the broken left turn and he jest plumb can't figger it out."

At which point, they would call their friends, who would come on over and pretty soon there would be a barbecue going and beer flowing and people talking and laughing and pointing at me. Eventually, one of them would come over and ask me what I was doing and I would have to admit that I couldn't figure out how to get my horse to the other side of the fence. They would take pity on me and lead it there, but only after another 10 minutes of pointing and laughing and taking family pictures next to The City Slicker Who Couldn't Ride Around the Fence.

Rather than risk this embarrassment, I focused my entire being on getting to the other side of the fence, even if it did involve a slight left turn. I spurred Flint on, engaged his faulty left turn mechanism, and managed to turn the few degrees necessary to complete the maneuver. Exhausted from the strain, I congratulated myself and waited for Karin.

She rode by, oblivious to both my skill and the disaster I had narrowly averted, and proceeded to do something completely and wholly irresponsible. She trotted. Or rather, Rocky trotted. But as I mentioned earlier, she had entered into some sort of evil conspiracy with him to make me look bad and could get him to do things like that. Several hundreds yards later, she stopped, turned and looked at me expectantly.

I turned and looked behind me in the hopes that there was a herd of buffalo about to trample me and that had caught her attention. Nothing. I would have to trot. I kicked Flint with my heels and clicked my tongue. I'm pretty sure all this meant to Flint was that his Sack-O-Potatoes Meter was functioning correctly because he continued to walk slowly up the road. I kicked again, clicked again and hit him with the stick, Animal Welfare people be damned. He trotted a few steps and returned to a walk.

I looked at Karin and grinned. She stared back. I kicked Flint again to convince him to trot, then kept kicking him. I had mistakenly assumed that horses were like cars—once you depress the accelerator enough to reach a certain speed, you don't have to depress it any further. Instead, horses are like old-fashioned pumps—stop moving the handle up and down and the water stops flowing. It was an awfully silly way to ride. Maybe it would tone my inner thighs.

When I reached Karin, she trotted alongside. Now that I'd mastered The Right Turn and Basic Equine Acceleration, she said, it was time to learn how to post. In a gallop, she explained, the horse's body stays relatively level. In consequence, so does the rider. This makes a gallop a comfortable if frightening experience.

Trotting, on the other hand, causes the horse's body to move up and down. This motion is translated to the rider and consequently trotting is a bone-jarring activity. With each step, the rider's body is thrown into the air and slammed back into the saddle. Although the saddle is made of leather, it has the same comfort and consistency as a grammar school chair. I wondered if they made padded saddles.

Posting was designed to alleviate the discomfort of trotting. It was quite simple, Karin explained. You picked one of the horse's shoulders—it didn't matter which one—and each time that shoulder moved forward, you stood up in your stirrups. I chose the right shoulder, assuming that the entire left side of Flint was as broken as his steering mechanism.

Karin demonstrated how graceful posting is. Like most things that look easy, it wasn't. It is bad enough to be trotting up a wide country road at four or five miles per hour with the certain conviction that you are going to fall off. To then divide your attention between an unfamiliar horse muscle and what you're going to hit when you fall off is an almost impossible situation.

Stand, sit, stand, sit, stand, sit—that part was easy. It was synchronizing my motion with Flint's that was hard. One moment, we would be in perfect harmony, and I would marvel at the grace and ease with which I posted. A moment later, I would fall a half phase behind and find myself lifting my body twice as high and hitting Flint's body twice as hard. I'm sure he disliked it, too, for he soon stopped trotting. I didn't argue.

The road curved past a cottage and climbed uphill. Karin and Rocky were at its top waiting for us. Embarrassed by our slow pace, I forced Flint to trot. As soon as Karin turned and trotted off, he slowed to a walk. He liked trotting no more than I did. Perhaps we had reached the same subtle communion as Rocky and Karin, but I doubt it. He wanted to nurse his sore leg and I wanted to nurse my sore butt.

The road flattened into a clearing where we met another party returning to the corral. I moved Flint off the side of the trail—to the right, of course—and let them go by. Some of them were trotting downhill at an alarming pace, and I hoped Karin wouldn't get any ideas. After the last of the horses thundered by, I tried once to move Flint back left onto the trail. As before, he refused to turn left so I turned him almost a full circle to the right to get back on the trail. Maybe it's his tie rod, I thought.

We continued uphill through a field dotted with aspens. The road split, and Karin purposely took the left fork. She pretended to be unaware of the obvious defect in my horse, but I was sure I felt a biting malevolence in her actions. Scare me climbing, they seemed to say. To spite her, I started my turn early and swung Flint to the left a stunning 10 degrees. Once again, she failed to notice.

The road climbed through a pine forest and forked again to the left. Several hundred feet of trotting, posting and bruising brought us to a short slope blocked at the bottom by a fallen tree. Karin walked her horse slowly toward it. This was a good sign, as I was fairly sure that a horse has to run before it jumps over something.

When Karin reached the tree, she did not turn around and come back as might have seemed sensible. Instead, she detoured to the left on a path blazed by other riders. The path passed dangerously close to a tree with low branches and I wondered if Flint knew the same rider-against-the-tree trick as Big Red.

Just as I emerged from the woods, Karin announced that the road was boring. We would return the way we had come and take another road that branched left and climbed up the steep hill behind us. As I passed the tree again, I considered whether Karin was trying to teach Flint how to strip me off. Ritual sacrifices seemed a bit much, even for Karin, but there was no telling just how far this mystical communion with the beast went.

Another session of trotting led back to the junction where we turned (left) and headed uphill. An overgrown path headed into bushy aspen trees on the right. Sensing another opportunity to get rid of me, Karin plunged into the thicket. When the path merged back into the road and Karin saw that I was still with her, she headed up a hill so steep it would make a Land Rover whimper.

One hundred feet later, with me almost hugging Flint's neck to keep from sliding off the back of the saddle, the road ran straight up what appeared to be the face of a cliff. I said that enough was enough. I was not taking Flint rock climbing. Karin smiled and pleasantly said, "OK." I was worried. Karin is never pleasant.

Sure enough, as soon as we headed downhill, Karin volunteered that this might be the steepest hill she had ever ridden down. Weren't hills dangerous? I asked. Most certainly, she replied. Horses were just as likely as people to trip while walking down a steep hill. Terrific, I thought. Here I am, leaning back as far as possible to avoid sliding over Flint's neck but not so far back as to bathe in his noxious gases, gripping the saddle horn like a complete rookie, and my horse is destined to trip.

A few moments later, Flint stumbled. It was that bum leg of his. I froze. Would we tumble down the hill like a snowball of cartoon characters, or would he simply land on me with a flat, final splat? Flint caught himself and continued down the hill. Certain I was about to die, I wondered if I should call to Karin and offer her a parting vow of love. Flint stumbled again. I forgot about parting vows and started planning where I would jump and exactly what trajectory I would need to avoid having a flatulent Toyota land on my head.

By this time, Karin had reached flatter ground and started making noises about trotting again. I didn't reply. Between Flint's constant stumbling and my imminent demise, I didn't have time to worry about trotting. Karin disappeared around a corner. When I miraculously reached gentler ground, I coaxed Flint into a trot but a stumble or two convinced me to shift him back into compound low. We caught up to Karin several minutes later.

"So, have you had enough? Or should we just keep going?" she asked in a voice I normally associated with the darkness behind a lamp in a bad cops-and-robbers movie. The words were innocent, but the question was freighted with malice.

"This is your thing. We'll stay out as long as you like," I squeaked back. My words were also freighted with unspoken meaning: I was trying my best to speak of abject surrender.

"We'll head back, then. That'll just make two hours."

She turned and shot off across a dangerous looking meadow. It was covered with grass, flowers and small bushes. I was worried that Flint would trip on them, and we carefully picked our way across. After several near misses with a buttercup, we came to the road. Karin had executed a graceful left turn here, but I was forced to spin 270 degrees to the right.

Karin and Rocky were up ahead somewhere, cantering away in horse heaven. Even Flint seemed happy—he had visions of Oats Benedict—and threatened to break into a celebratory trot. I reined him in and considered throwing out the saddle as a sea anchor when Karin yelled that we had 20 minutes left. I allowed Flint his trot until we reached the top of the final hill.

As I gazed over its lip, I remembered how Flint had stumbled on the last hill and considered my options. Unlike many sport utility vehicles, Flint lacked a winch, and a quick check of his saddlebags failed to produce a tow cable with which I could lower him. That left his four-wheel drive, which I already knew to be faulty. Cursing myself for renting the cheapie model, I put him into compound low and edged us into the abyss.

Karin had already reached the level ground and abandoned any pretense of riding with me. She raced Rocky across the flats at a full gallop. Her long brown hair streamed wildly behind her as she crouched over the saddle. Where the road turned toward the highway, she wheeled Rocky around. Rocky's head tossed in the air and his lungs heaved from the exertion.

I glanced at Flint, then back at Karin. I knew she wanted us to share her exhilaration. *Gallop*, her face said. Gallop. For a second time, Flint and I entered into that forthright bond between man and horse. We looked deep into our hearts and summoned up an answer to Karin's challenge. "What? Are you absolutely inSANE!?" it screamed. Flint trotted a short distance and gave up completely.

Karin trotted out to meet me. We had a few minutes left and she insisted we ride back up the road. This time, even Rocky disagreed and we had to wrestle the horses to point them away from the corral. I soon found that the only way I could make any progress was to turn Flint a hair to the left, let him turn back to the right, then continue to spin him another 180 degrees. Momentarily disoriented, he would take a few steps in the correct direction before he discovered he'd been had and started the whole process over again.

We continued in this manner, spinning like a drunken top, for a 100 feet or so, by which time I was on the wrong side of the fence that had given me such troubles on the way out. Relieved that the farmer didn't show up to laugh and that Karin was having similar troubles, I suggested we give up. I saw little point in angering Flint to the point of bucking me off and trampling me into little road apples. Karin agreed.

Flint's attitude improved famously with each step closer to home. I had almost convinced myself that I was in control when we met two young girls along the fence line. I pulled Flint far off the trail so that he wouldn't disturb their horses. Although this struck me as the proper thing to do, it struck the girls as odd and they regarded me like they might someone talking to a lamppost. They ventured a polite hello and rode quickly on.

As Flint and I executed a final right-hand pirouette to rejoin the trail, I thought about the girls. They couldn't have been much more than 9 or 10 years old, yet they seemed to have complete control over their horses. It was almost as if some subtle connection bound them, something that transcended the differences in age, sex and species. I wondered if the Horse Chow Division of the Ralston-Purina Co. had gotten to them, too.

Bear Necessities

By Frank Krajcovic

The most embarrassing thing I've ever done in the woods was so embarrassing that I'm sure as hell not going to tell you about it. But after that, the second worst thing was getting conned by a smooth-talking salesman and walking out of his store with what he advertised as the world's most advanced emergency bear bite kit.

It turned out that it was nothing but a snake bite kit with the word "snake" crossed out and the word "bear" written in its place. But I was young, naive and had never seen a bear in my life except for an old snapshot of one in which the bear had to have been at least 600 yards away. The bear looked no bigger than a cricket; and if you had told me that bears go courting by rubbing their legs together on cold evenings, I would have been none the wiser.

So imagine my complete shock when, while walking through the woods with the woman whom I was convinced I would stay with for life, a woman who had never seen me do a thing or even imagined me doing a thing that did not include the most advanced stages of bravery (she had seen me knock chips off of shoulders I could barely reach, and dive from high rocks into pools of water a basset would have trouble wallowing in), imagine walking with this woman and having her shriek in her most "Oh-please-help-me-I'm-so-helpless" way, "EEEP, a bear!"

I responded with something reassuring, like, "Relax, darling, leave it to me." I whipped out my Swiss Army Knife and advanced, poking in the grass with my boot, expecting at any time to turn up the rascal who had so alarmed my woman.

Finally, I detected some movement, then realized I was face-to-face with the knee of a bear.

That was the other major surprise of the afternoon: bears stand up. This bear was standing up, staring at me and snarling a challenge which, near as I could translate, was, "I want the dame."

If this was a make-believe story, I would have gotten on my tip-toes and snarled right back, "Well, she's mine, and you can't have her."

But the truth of the matter is that I couldn't have summoned up a snarl if I'd had a committee of 10 working on it. My mouth went dry. My pants went wet. I bit my tongue in order to hold back some snide remark about how gosh-awful his breath was. (I think the actual comment I bit back was: "What have you been eating? The intestines of a long deceased goat?") Then, I fainted—or ad-libbed a heart attack or something. Whatever it was, I hit the ground with a thud and had a bump on my head to prove it.

When I woke up, the bear was gone. So was Elaine. One of only two things could have happened, neither of which was going to make me gush over with pleasure. Either I had done a real poor job of protecting Elaine, and the larger than expected bear had made a mid-day snack of her, and all the king's horses and all the king's men and even my emergency bear bite kit wouldn't have been able to put her back together again; or she had escaped and made it back to town and was now in Rosie's, bending her elbow with whomever would buy her a drink, and making arrangements for me to be the town laughingstock for at least the rest of the century. Elaine was not the type of woman to show sympathy toward perceived acts of cowardice.

It was a choice of returning to a place where everyone was convinced that I was an idiot, or moving to a town where folks had not yet made up their minds. A simple choice if there ever was one. I sold my bear bite kit as soon as I was able to. I'm writing this from a vastly different town under an assumed name. If you're able to somehow figure out who I am, please don't tell my neighbors, OK?

Liontrek

By Peter Stapleton

I kept saying, "Yeah, Dan, a hike sounds real good." I even read the damn trail description and said, "Yeah, Dan, that hike sounds real good." Thirteen miles, with something like a steam trunk/backpack strapped to my body, up and then down a mountain. Hell, two miles, stripped of all weight except a brand new pair of socks, on ground flat enough to qualify as a pool table, and I'm sweating like Jehovah on the sixth day. So what drove me to accept this invitation, and from a redhead to boot, reputed to be the most unstable of all the hair colors?

I did indeed pause to reflect on this question, but at a point that was probably too late—sliding down the mountainside, alone, following the closest thing to a trail I could discern and feeling all the energy of a 72-year-old man with but a thin pint of blood left in his arteries.

Oh, things were fine at first, camping near the trailhead on the eve of departure. The stars were bright and plenty, reminding me of the closest thing I'd come to at that point in my life—a planetarium. It seemed fabricated. After crawling into my own tent, I heard the nocturnal crowd around us swinging into their predatory workaday. Sure, that spooked me for a second, and my eyes were wide for a bit. Funny thing about icy, bloodless fear, though—it can surely make time crawl. It seemed like I was awake for seven or eight hours, when, in reality, it was probably only six! But, contrary to what my mind had begun to assert, alert for hours and feeding on itself, the sun did find us in our little clearing and had not moved on to a more appreciative solar system. It's those small comforts...

So we packed up, located the trailhead and strapped the great green monkeys to our back. Truthfully now, and I don't mean to brag, the pack added no more weight than a plain white T-shirt. But Dan finally talked me into filling it with more than an extra pair of socks and the two Homer Simpson dolls strapped on the outside for protection. It was good to have someone with a bit of outdoors experience along, someone who could suggest items like food,

water—even a sleeping bag. I might have looked quite the fool out on the trail. So I stuffed my pack full like a Christmas stocking, and began the ascent, humorously thinking of myself as that plucky little puppy who served as the whole of the Grinch's sled team as the fiend attempted to thieve the holiday from the innocent Whos populating Whoville. Except my Grinch had red hair, not green, and moved like a guilty weasel every time I attempted to plant my pack rightfully on his back.

A mile or so up the narrow trail, however, a beautiful green vista opened itself to our eyes and banished, for quite a while, my colorful cartoon hallucinations which had disturbed Dan for the first hour of our walk. He even considered returning my Swiss Army knife. The first and steepest of the climbs was over. The trail synopsis assured us that a period of "gentle, undulating hills" was ahead, before the path dropped us like fragile eggs into Church Creek Divide. The path was, indeed, gentle as described, only much of it wound along a very grassy mountainside steep enough to furnish a blindingly quick ride to the bottom. I watched my boots quite a bit during this segment to ensure they did not stray from the actual path, which was about three inches long and peppered, jokingly, I am sure, with rocks round as golf balls capable of shifting a misplaced foot into all sorts of unpredictable positions. Imagine our mirth!

But the scenery was undeniably breathtaking, and we eventually found the Church Creek Divide, a four-way junction just above the Carmel River that was suggested by the trail book as an opportune campsite. We decided to press on, however, and I was even sincere about continuing to pick my feet up and set them down.

A lone hiker, who began the trail not long after us, passed us by, taking the opposite direction of the loop we would soon be on. Logically, we should have met later, in the middle of the circle, but he appeared to vanish. Perhaps the hike became too much and he simply turned back, or perhaps he avoided meeting us again because he felt guilty about something—like maybe the theft of a Homer doll that had been lashed to my backpack like some kind of superstitious icon. I submit this to the reader: I entered the Ventana Wilderness with two such dolls, but when I finally found my way out and back to the car, there remained only one Homer.

As the afternoon settled in on the first day of our journey, Dan and I found ourselves climbing and crawling over and under fallen trees that we were lucky to encounter, being the first on this particular trail after months of heavy rains. As we pushed through each obstacle, we congratulated ourselves on being so fortuitous as to find the wilderness in a truly wild state. Ah, but the sarcasm soon wore thin, and we went back to cursing our fate.

For a while, the hike was pretty level, carrying us, at times, alongside steep, high banks on the Carmel River. Eventually, thankfully, the descent began, a series of insidious switchbacks that would bring us in to Pine Valley camp, where we could spend the night before completing the last leg of our course the next day.

When the day had begun, and we climbed, scaled and ascended for approximately 25 hours, I smiled, when I was able to, singing somewhat painfully to myself, "What goes up, must come down...." It was not a pretty song, but I had somehow grabbed hold of the deluded notion that after enduring this Aztec staircase of a climb, I would be justly rewarded when it finally peaked and I could literally say, "Well, Dan, its all downhill from here...." I would giggle then, and let gravity assist me gingerly down the mountainside.

Someone shoulda slapped me hard with the way I was thinking. Dan tried to tell me at the beginning, claiming "downhills were almost as tough as uphills." I dismissed it right off, of course, assuming it was some kind of bizarre reverse psychology intended to make me get sweet on the idea of uphills. That's the moment I needed a good backhand slap across my face, delivering me back into reality. I started that downhill and gravity, as it turns out, had no understanding of the adverb "gingerly." As the descent began in earnest, the sum of the march to this point was making itself well known in all sorts of muscle groups throughout my body. My joints groaned and my knees sang an ugly blues through each step. I had been rationing my water wisely, but my lithium was stealing every drop, like a drunk on Sunday.

I was as thirsty as Dan, and I sat down for a moment, but found my water bottles were only shallow backwash by then. My lithium, prescribed only to stabilize mood swings, decided to go "above and beyond" the job description and devised a method of converting energy and sense of judgment into fluid for consumption. It could continue its precarious duty of balancing the shifty forces of yin and yang, while I could pretty much stop thinking straight. Foolishly I welcomed this mental haze and told Dan to go ahead, as I would need just a small amount of rest. "Maybe six hours, Dan—you know, just a quick nap."

He began down the trail while I sat against a rock, wondering how I might move. But as I realized that camp held water, and I, coincidentally, needed water like J. Edgar needed Clyde, I resolved to follow Dan to the promised land. Things went well, too, following the switchbacks that cut side to side across the mountain. Until the moment, of course, when I discovered I was not following any trail, and probably hadn't been for at least 20 minutes. The haze had apparently interceded at some point back, and, for its own nebulous reasons, chose to omit the trail turn from its signals to my consciousness. I basically zigged when I shoulda zagged.

I should have backtracked, I know. I did think of it, but since I'd been heading more or less downhill for 20 minutes, my legs balked at any climb. Then, fortunately, or so I believed, eyeing my position dejectedly, I spotted tracks in the leafy dirt. Oh joy! Perhaps this was the path, a bit weathered, and these were Dan's boot prints in the dirt! I practically skipped with my full load for another 20 minutes until the continuing absence of a clear trail gripped my mind. But these must be Dan's tracks—there was no one else out here and— oh. I blushed when it suddenly became clear that I'd mistaken the obvious prints of a mountain lion for Dan's.

And with another half second of mostly cloudless thought, I surmised I was following the cat.

Now I recalled, in some detail, the *Reader's Digests* I used to read as a child on rainy weekends. Sure, there was "Laughter is the Best Medicine," but my attention was always on the latest "Drama in Real Life." Now I believed I might be writing my own harrowing encounter with nature, from a hospital bed most likely, explaining to all how I'd shrewdly diverted the attention of this beast by shoving my leg between its jaws.

I yelled loudly for Dan, but with no answer I realized the unpopulated land I had lost myself on was vast, uncompromising and probably contained snakes.

"Can't always be worrying about the reptiles," I told myself, forgetting 25 years of a severe serpent-phobia. I plunged further down, hoping to find a trail, a sign, maybe even a body (live, I mean). The ground was steep and buried beneath thick blankets of wet leaves and rotting tree parts. Each step dropped me another 6 feet down, tripping me up often and covering my clothes in dirt. Finally I stopped, suddenly understanding what the sound I heard meant. I was near the river. It must be the Carmel, I cleverly guessed. According to the trail description, our planned campground was on the Carmel. I once again lifted the heavy pack and edged sideways, closer to the sweet music of running water.

A few adolescent years serving time in the Boy Scouts taught me almost nil, but I did remember reading a couple survival tips dealing with losing oneself in the great outdoors. "Consumption of shoe leather can provide nutrition." I grew nauseous at that and recalled another maxim, "Find water and follow it downstream." So I slid down the bank toward the relatively shallow river. Before hitting the water, however, I paused to change into my old running shoes, a pair

I'd tied to my pack in the event trail conditions had me worried about ruining my new boots. With that done, I started downstream, unable to walk the tree-thick banks. Soon my legs were wet to about my knees, but the cool water felt good. The momentary burst my body had afforded me with the wet discovery was draining quickly, however, and when I neared the top of 15-foot waterfall, I lost hope and dropped myself onto a small patch of dry ground.

The sun was leaving, and I wondered if I might actually have to sleep with wildcats that night. Quenching my thirst might help me think a little straighter, so I pulled out my water filter and pumped about a gallon of cool water from the stream. After drinking half of that and eating an energy bar, I decided to continue my waterwalk. But the pack was too much at this point. The sun slipped another notch and I admitted to myself the pack, though expensive, was just "stuff." Working against the waning sun, I detached the top, a well-designed hip pouch, and filled it with the bare essentials. I tied the main bag to a tree and left a short note to anyone who may find it.

I slid crazily down the small falls and kept moving. With my load lightened considerably, my progress was better, my mood hopeful.

Fifteen to 20 minutes forward, the river was blocked by the thick trunks of several fallen trees. I climbed to the bank, then over the first tree. Standing on that wood, I tried another call, and nearly fell over when I heard another voice.

"Dan!" A second call was answered, and I moved haphazardly in the direction of the voice. Moments later, I was kissing the semi-sweet ground of the small clearing like some kind of Pope Lewis N. Clark XVI until Dan, employing a bit of foresight, dragged me from the patch of poison oak I'd chosen to express my oral gratitude on.

He promised to cook the dinner, and the phantom smell of my dehydrated enchiladas gave me the inspiration I needed to make a quick run back up the river for my backpack.

I even had a moment to enjoy a cold bath of sorts in the clear, shallow river that had delivered me from evil. Looking back, I'm comfortably sure that the liquid enchiladas I stuffed myself with that night probably tasted like wet cardboard—bad wet cardboard. But the manna then was truly dropped from on high, and I slept hard, no dreams, save for one. In it, I'd somehow strayed from the trail and....

Final Vision

By Michael Hancock

There I was, hanging on the edge of a glacier, my legs dangling above a thousand feet of open air, supported only by the tip of my ice axe. Just moments before, I was reveling in the accomplishment of having scaled my highest peak yet. Deedee and I were completing our descent, just a couple of hours from our base camp, when all hell broke loose. Despite my current personal predicament, my mind was racing over what had just occurred, including my last vision of Deedee tumbling uncontrollably over the glacier's edge, and the terrifying silence that followed.

This climb had been a goal of mine for years. I grew up reading the adventures of all the great mountaineers, and imagined myself climbing in vertical landscapes of snow and ice on the high points of the world. Now I never seriously thought I'd really climb Everest or K2, but I wanted to at least make an ascent of one of the lesser, but still impressive, substitutes—the volcanoes of the Cascade Range. Baker, Adams, Hood, Rainier, Shasta. Only about half as high as the Himalayas, but still a challenge, and just as magical. Raised in the shadow of the northern Appalachians, I've experienced the fierce weather conditions and arctic terrain of Mount Washington. I've hung by my fingertips on the rocky faces of many eastern mountains, and even climbed in the thin air of California's Sierra Nevada. But I yearned to combine these experiences and walk the high glaciers of a serious mountain. The time had arrived.

As my wife and I set up our tent in a snowfield at 10,000 feet on Mount Shasta—the southernmost of the resting Cascade volcanoes—my mind was racing with excitement. Although we were about to attempt ascending the peak via a much less technically challenging route than I'd experienced on other mountains, the thrill of knowing that I would soon be walking and climbing the monstrous icy slopes of this breathtaking mountain was overwhelming. Not only would I experience the thrill of climbing on a huge Cascade volcano, but I would be visiting the peak of a mountain believed by many to be one of the most spiritual hot spots in the world!

Through all my excitement, I had to continually remind myself that I would be attempting this climb with my wife, a native of Florida who grew up in the shadow of orange and grapefruit trees. Although Deedee was certainly in shape for the climb, her experience in using crampons and an ice axe was limited. We met several climbing parties at base camp that had failed to reach the summit that day due to altitude sickness, but we were reassured by the climbers that our chosen route was not technically difficult. Although we should be cautious and watch the weather, we should have no trouble at all if we were acclimatized to the high elevation. This sounded great to me, because after all, it wasn't a physical challenge I was looking for, it was the experience of being on top of this massive mountain.

As an afterthought, however, we were warned that we should be off the mountain as soon as possible, because our chosen route was susceptible to falling rocks and ice as the temperature rises late in the day.

"No problem," I reassured Deedee. "Piece of cake."

Or so I thought, despite the several warning signs that followed. The spirit of the mountain may have been warning us, but we chose to ignore it. We had climbed to our base camp under an azure sky, but ominous thunderclouds rolled in and presented an awesome lightning show on the glaciers above. Throughout much of the night a vicious storm of rain and hail raged, and between the excitement of the next day's climb and the fear of our tent collapsing in the high wind and pelting rain, neither of us slept much. Even though the storm passed, and we awoke to a crisp calm morning, we heard the low roar of an avalanche on the upper slopes.

We were reminded how powerful this mountain can be, but quickly got started on our adventure. A final sign of trouble was realized when my brand new camera decided to seize up as I attempted to photograph Deedee loaded down with her newly donned climbing equipment. Damn. Why had I talked myself into leaving my backup camera ("old trusty") in the car on one of our biggest adventures?

The next several hours of climbing were spectacular. It was July, but the air was cold. The remaining packed snow on the glaciers was firm, and climbing was easy. Although a bit overcautious on the 40-degree pitch of the lower snowfields, Deedee was smiling from ear to ear as we weaved our way through the rock and ice. Heavy clouds blanketed the mountain top, so the visibility was poor, but I knew the cold air would allow us a leisurely round-trip to the summit, leaving plenty of time to explore before we returned to our base camp.

Despite our early start, the more experienced climbers we met the day before soon passed us, after stopping to discuss how perfect a climbing day we all had. Deedee joked that we were going to try to reach the summit before dark, but we knew we had plenty of time. Before long, we had reached a spectacular rock formation covered with snow and ice—what we expected to be the only potentially challenging section of our climb (challenging at our level of climbing anyway). The rock formation is theorized to be the lower limit of one of the most recent lava flows from Mount Shasta, and consists of several hundred feet of rock face bracketed by even steeper drops down to yet more glaciers. It can be passed by one of two ways: climbing directly over the rock; or a long climb around the formation, part of which involves crossing a large and dangerous bergschrund (a crevasse formed where the glacier is pulling away from the rock).

Choice number one was certainly the quickest route, and hardly a challenge for an experienced climber, but the route did involve some rather steep and exposed climbing. We weren't carrying climbing ropes, but because of the cold air, I guessed that the rock would have firm, easy-to-climb snow and ice, so Deedee agreed to attempt the shortcut. As I suspected, the snow was crunchy, climbing was easy, and before long we were back on firm snow and pushing toward the summit. The indigo-blue glaciers, coupled with the enveloping clouds, the steaming vents and the bizarre rock formations surrounding the ancient crater, provided a hauntingly beautiful scene.

The high point of the summit consisted of a jumble of rocks rising 200 feet over the crater, across the large summit from where we stood. The hike across the ice-filled crater was unworldly, and when we finally scrambled up to the highest point, 14,162 feet above sea level, we hugged each other in celebration of our accomplishment. I was proud that Deedee had toughed out the climb, and also thrilled to be looking out over such an impressive landscape. Visibility was poor and the winds began to increase, so we had the summit to ourselves as we lingered at the top to soak up the incredible scene from our lonely perch.

After some time had passed, I became somewhat concerned about the lateness of the day. It was already high noon, and I knew we should be off the snow and glaciers before the heat of the day began melting the surface of the ice and increasing the likelihood of rock falls. Additionally, the visibility was decreasing while the wind was increasing. Although it had warmed somewhat throughout the day, it was still very cold on the summit, and the potential for rock falls was minimal. Just the same, I suggested we move on.

The climb down was much slower than I had guessed. Although we had plenty of daylight, it had already been a long day, and the thin air and exertion were beginning to take their toll. The temperature was not noticeably rising, but the visibility was deteriorating, and I was anxious to return to our base camp. Deedee was moving slowly, and I had to wait for longer and longer periods of time for her to catch up with me. She began looking very troubled, and I was concerned about how the high elevation might be affecting her.

As several hours passed, I was becoming more anxious to get off the glaciers, and began thinking of a way to recharge Deedee's energy level and increase her pace. As I slogged through the deep snow incised by the day's climbers, it dawned on me that there was an easier and more fun way—glissading. I demonstrated to Deedee that by sitting down, and using her ice axe as a brake, you could zip down the snowfields as on a toboggan. The bottom of the trail had become rather icy as the snow had melted during the day and refroze, while the sides of the trail were still unpacked powder. Cautious at first, she was soon flying down the mountain, laughing and looking as though she had done this all her life. I already knew Deedee was a better skier than me, despite her warm weather upbringing, but not this. This was my sport! Nevertheless, the fun gave her a second wind, and soon she had passed me and was out of sight. I caught up with Deedee at the top of a steep rock formation, where she was grinning from ear to ear.

"Let's do that again!" she joked.

I was happy to see that she was enjoying herself, and reassured that we'd have no problem returning to our base camp before dark. Although it was late in the day, the temperature was dropping, and the threat of rock fall would be minimal. My calm was quickly transformed to uneasiness as I peered down the rock we had climbed just hours before. Apparently the temperature at this elevation had been much warmer than at the summit, and the snow had melted and refroze throughout the course of the day. The path was coated with thick glare ice, and in some areas collapsed to tunnels of still unfrozen torrents below the packed snow. I initially considered pursuing the long haul around the rock formation, and descending across the bergschrund, but with the lateness of the day, I quickly discarded the idea.

I was uneasy about descending over the ice-covered rock unroped, but found that I had no trouble cutting steps with my ice axe, or even just the edge my crampons. With Deedee's new found strength, we could be through this segment in minutes, and the base camp would soon be in sight. Deedee was agreeable, and seemed very unconcerned, so we began our descent. The step cutting was easy, and we quietly progressed downward, enjoying the crisp cold, but foggy air. Before long, the end was in sight, and I began thinking back on our adventure.

Mountaineering can best be described with one word—balance. Of course, in the most literal sense, a climber must maintain good physical balance, but, maybe more important, must always maintain a mental balance. The success of many of the greatest attempts on the most challenging peaks of the world has often rested on the ability of the participants to meet the mental challenge of such feats. Many of these attempts have failed, not necessarily because of a lack of physical ability, but due to mental fatigue, loss of focus, loss of concentration. Through reading the annals of the great climbers, and through my own experience, I've learned that climbing is not only a test of physical ability, but a test of mental ability, including overcoming fear, overcoming false constraints and being able to remain focused. Because of the obvious physical danger that always exists, despite our level of comfort or experience with any particular situation, the climber must always remain focused. Focus is necessary not only to accomplish the goal of reaching the summit, but to accomplish the goal of a safe return. In climbing, losing focus for one moment can spell disaster.

So when Deedee unknowingly placed a foot flat on glare ice rather than in one of my cut steps, disaster struck. The clang of metal on ice first broke the silence. Without any other warning, something from behind swept my feet from under me, and the flash of blue nylon immediately told me that it was my wife. By instinct, I grabbed a handful of the nylon with one hand, and rolled in an attempt to self arrest with my ice axe in the other hand. In desperation, I swung my axe with all my strength into the slope, but it simply bounced off the solid ice. Immediately, I swung again, and again, and again. Finally, the point of the axe dug deep, jolting us to a sudden stop. Very sudden. So sudden, the jolt of the stop was too much for my loose grip on the slick nylon of Deedee's jacket. With my feet dangling off the side of the formation, I watched as she continued in an uncontrollable slide down an icy channel, over the edge, and out of sight.

Not a shout, not a call, not a scream had been emitted by either of us during our mutual fall, and not a sound came from either of us now. The silence was terrifying. Still in the grip of the initial shock of what had just occurred, I stared up and down the rock. Although we had practiced the procedure for self arrest, Deedee had apparently dropped her axe in her panic before attempting to stop herself. I could see her ice axe lying on its side 30 feet up slope from me. We had fallen twice that distance, and Deedee continued for 60 more feet before leaving my field of sight. Without an ice axe, she would have little to no chance of stopping herself, and with a 40-degree icy slope below the rock formation, she could continue gathering speed until something finally stopped her—suddenly and hard.

My mind raced as I struggled not to panic. "Deeeeee deeeeee," I finally cried, but my shouts were answered by silence. I stared at the lonely ice axe above, and some time passed before the initial shock wore off and I realized my personal predicament. Had my axe not held, my fate would have been certain. I had slipped down a side channel in the ice, and stopped short of taking a plunge down an 80-degree slope (for those readers who missed high school geometry, this is otherwise known as a cliff). At least most of me had. I kicked my feet toward the slope, but my crampons would not grip. I pulled hard on the ice axe, praying that it would hold. It did, and I secured myself on the channel bottom.

As my mind began to clear, fear set in, and I again was unable to move. Gathering myself, I stood, and began taking a small step downward. Pain shot through my side as I placed my weight on my right leg, and looking down, I saw a tear in my climbing pants stretching from my knee to my ankle, probably torn from a flailing crampon. The long gash beneath was deep but tolerable. I began my descent, and shortly realized that I needed to retrieve Deedee's ice axe, which she would need when I found her. I labored up slope to the second axe, and then turned back downward.

Struggling to block all the possible consequences from my mind, and using both ice axes for support, I moved as quickly as I could. In minutes I reached the rock's edge. Mouth agape, I peered over. Nothing. The visibility was no more than 20 feet, and there was no sign of Deedee. The surface of the snow was hard and icy, and although the tracks of previous climbers (all well below us now) were visible, I saw no signs of Deedee's descent. I called out, but my shouts were lost in the now howling wind and went unanswered.

Now in near panic, I began half climbing, half falling down the slope. Still using both axes, I pushed on as fast as I could. If she was badly hurt, or unconscious, it would take me many hours to carry her just to the base camp. It would be several hours from there to the car, and then some time to drive to the closest phone for help. With the sun low on the horizon, darkness would soon be here, bringing with it bitter cold. The decreasing visibility could be a warning sign of a storm similar to the one we had the previous night, which would make a bad situation much worse. If she were badly hurt, or... I had to calm down and move on as fast as I could.

Minutes seemed like hours as I pushed on, constantly scanning the surrounding area. "Deeeeee deeeeeee ....Deeeeee deeeeeee," constantly shouting, panicking. "Deeeee deeeeee ......Deeeeee deeeeee." Fifteen, 20 minutes...nothing, nothing! "Deeeeee deeeee" ...wait! Did I hear a response, or my own echo? "Deeeee deeee?"

"I'm here," came a muffled reply. Below I could see a small figure, quickly approaching from below.

Near exhaustion and near panic, we both collapsed on one another and embraced. Shaking, but in otherwise perfect health, Deedee told me of her long, but otherwise uneventful slide down the snowfield, which ended by bogging down in a snowdrift.

"The slide was no problem," she explained. "The problem was my fear for you!"

Apparently, the last vision she had before sliding over the edge of the ice chute was of me sliding over the edge of the cliff. Fearing the worst, she had made her way around near the cliff bottom. Seeing nothing, she quickly began ascending up the snowfield toward the rock formation, until we found each other. We still had a long way to go, and with torn jackets and bleeding legs, we carefully headed down toward base camp. We nervously began joking about the fall, but in our minds we knew we had learned a major lesson about both climbing and the priority of values in our lives.

Our expensive climbing gear was torn, but as we sat safely in our car, hand in hand, we realized how extremely inexpensive our lesson had been.

Killer Swans From Hell

By Lindsay Koehler

No shit! There I was—on a four-day kayaking trip down the Delaware River, my first overnight river trip, and actually my first paddling trip of any length. I worried about the weather, worried about wrist strain (remembering horror stories of the grinding, crunching sounds which occur when beginners overtax themselves), really worried about the rapids at legendary Skinner's Falls (where "an average of six people die every year," or so they say), and wondered whether I was tough enough to keep up with my husband, Dan, and our friend, Jim, who were in sleeker, more appropriate kayaks. (My boat falls into the inglorious class of "playboat"—and even I don't take it too seriously.)

I was giving the river all kinds of respect, on the other hand. The Delaware is not known as extremely technical water, but the very first section we would run was classed "not for beginners" in all the guidebooks. By the rapids rating system, the toughest we would face was a Class II, but all the experts suggest adding an additional danger level if the water falls below 55 degrees and they tack on another level for the spring flood. It was the beginning of May—and both these qualifications applied. Great. I could just imagine the walls of water the Class IV rapids would hurl onto my head. Then I'd go under, never to resurface, trapped in a funnel or strainer, and the first question everyone would ask, "On the Delaware? The Delaware River? She died on a river in New Jersey? Oh." Yeah, that image really made me feel positive.

My previous yaking experience had been limited to Class I ponds and streams—but I'm in pretty good shape, and how bad could this be, I rationalized. I've been dumped before, and as long as I had dry clothes to put on, I've always been OK.

When it rains straight for four days and three nights, though, not much stays dry; and camping outside when nighttime temperatures fall down around freezing gets a lot less comfortable when it's pour-

Sanders, '96

ing rain. But, surprisingly, everything was going pretty well. All my shorter river and lake trips in the kayak had paid off, and wrist strain wasn't a problem. Even the rain and cold was bearable, and I'm usually the first one to grab long johns when everyone else is wearing shorts. No, the problem which blindsided me, for which I hadn't prepared and which I will dread on all future paddling trips, came in a very different shape—that of a 40-pound waterfowl, to be specific.

Yes, the demon that terrorizes my nightmares these days takes the shape of a truly evil, malicious, nasty, aggressive, powerful, kayak-hating swan (and its mate, who was even meaner).

People who live around ponds will not be surprised to hear about a kayak-chasing bird. Heck, anyone who's gone to a goose-infested public park to "feed the ducks" may have seen geese hiss and shake their wings around—but swans are a completely different story. These swans, in particular, did not come from eggs like most feathered beasts. No—these were spawned from the very mouth of Hell, with a mission to not just protect their specially selected nesting spot, but to scare the bejesus out of any boater within a mile's radius.

You could conjecture that they were only proud plumed parents, defending their cygnets-to-be from fierce, boat-borne invaders (in our playboats). But no shit, I was there, and I can tell you that these swans had fire in their eyes and attack on their minds. Simple defense against nonthreatening kayakers in the requisite silly hats on a rainy day would require some wing flapping and maybe a well-timed hiss, but these buggers chased us for more than a mile.

We had been lulled into a false sense of security farther upriver, when, rounding a bend in the river, we saw a nesting pair. We had been told by some local fisherman that the swans could be defensive, and we were advised to keep to the far side of the bank, which we did, without incident. It was after a Class I rapid in a shallow spot a bit further down where we entered the militarized swan zone.

Dan and I had passed through the rapid, and were waiting for Jim to clear off a submerged rock (as chef and chief provisioner, he carried most of the grub, so he rode lower in the water), when we heard the first hiss. Looking over my shoulder, I saw two swans paddling upriver. Against the current. And they were picking up speed. Putting their backs into it, so to speak. Really working up a swan sweat.

Having battled Skinner's Falls, near-freezing temperatures and three days of rain, it honestly didn't worry me.

Oh, for the innocence of ignorance! I had turned away from them to check on Jim's progress, so my back was to them during the first rush. The swooping, splashing sound was my first clue that I was about to be winged. When the swan hit me, I experienced some confusion. The most graceful of waterfowl, symbol of beauty and serenity—and it was attacking me? Wow. I turned down river and started paddling as fast as I could. Flight was foremost on my mind; fight had not a particle of real estate in my brain to call its own.

The paddling and the flow of the water carried me past the swan—whew, I was safe. I thought. I looked back to see the swan backpedaling, maintaining position. Calm. Calculating. Letting me know I was its target and should prepare to meet my maker. Then it puffed up its chest, fanned out its wings and pulled its neck down onto its back—hissing. Swans, as you may be thinking, are not huge animals, it is true, but in a kayak you're eye-to-beady-eye with them, and they're in their natural element. Fear crept into my gut, and my adrenaline was pumping. The bird flapped its wings, rising up out of the water and half flew, half ran across the water directly at me. The wake this bird threw off would have done credit to a Donzi.

What to do? There was no way I could outrun it, not at that speed. Hitting it with my paddle didn't occur to me just yet, though it would soon. I tensed up, and waited. The closer it got, the louder the sound of its wings cutting the air became. It gets pretty loud right before it hits you, like a slowed-down, magnified heartbeat. Oh, maybe that was my heartbeat. Anyway, it was loud.

Shaken, but not hurt or tipped over, I checked my hair for white feathers. Seriously. I was still feeling the impact. When I got the guts to look, the swan's mate was preparing for another assault. By now, I was paddling like mad, but the swooping got louder and louder, and I was winged again. I found out later that Dan swung at the swan with his paddle, but it kept coming. (Animal rights people, be damned; this was self-defense!)

All the time, remember, the flow of the river was carrying us farther and farther down river, and you can't tell me a normal swan's personal nesting ground covers more than a mile. These two had a vendetta.

Dan pointed out that if I kept paddling at top speed, we'd leave Jim to face the fowl gauntlet alone, so we let the boats drift. The swans double-teamed us, one attacking and the other hanging back, rushing in when the attacker had passed to cover us. I've never been so intimidated by birds in my life. Finally, Jim caught up, keeping to the far side of the river, and we crossed the invisible boundary out of the militarized swan zone.

The experience has marked me in more ways than one. I've had arguments with swan- and waterfowl-lovers about the legal implications of braining birds with a paddle. Some of my friends now eye me funny when we walk past the ducks in the park—like I'm planning a counterattack. And I can't pass a swan-shaped lawn ornament without speeding up a little—even if I'm driving. Look around next time you go out: they're everywhere!

Pirates Of The Colorado

By Brian D. Whitmer

In yet another of my misguided attempts to suck the marrow from the proverbial bone of life, I find myself ranging the banks of the Colorado River where it passes through the very deepest section of the Grand Canyon. This time I'm seeking adventure in what most people consider to be the classic river trip—the one against which all others are measured—the one-week pontoon boat ride on the mighty rapids of the Colorado. Now...if only I could find the guys who are supposed to be leading the trip.

My companion, Carolyn, and I have spent the entire morning hiking down to this point from the south rim of the canyon, and we're a little perturbed that none of the folks milling around the beached rafts is waving us over with a smile and a welcome. Several rafting companies seem to be represented here, however, and there's no telling the passengers from the company boatmen. They all look a bit gamy, if you ask me.

When we finally find our trip leader, he turns out to be soft-spoken and friendly, but doesn't instill much confidence. He speaks slowly, with something of a surfer's drawl, and is the very definition of "laid back." We suspect he's on Quaaludes.

We learn from a quick orientation that our group of 24 will be divided between two large pontoon boats traveling together. There will be two professional boatmen on each raft, one driver and one crewman. Granted, their appearance is what you'd expect of guys who've been on the river for a full week already, which they have; still, I can't help thinking that they look a little smelly and disheveled to be calling themselves "professionals."

Carolyn and I jump on a boat, not yet knowing who will pilot it. Our trip leader, Quaalude boy, takes command of the other boat and steers it into the current. The driver of our boat follows. Our driver has classic good looks. Given a shave and a shirt, he could probably be a movie star. Carolyn schmoozes with him at every opportunity, as does every other woman on the boat.

Less than three minutes after climbing aboard, we're already splashing through some small rapids. For a desert river, the Colorado is unbelievably cold. A little bow spray comes over the front and several shots of icy water splash up from below, squirting up our thighs through the gap between the pontoons. I let out an unsuppressible hoot and look uneasily at Carolyn, who is also wide-eyed and shocked by the temperature of the water. The boatmen, way in the back and shielded from the spray by us and our gear, are warm and dry. Grinning devilishly, our driver asks if any of us would like a cool drink. We wring out our shirts and decline. "The water here's only about 48 degrees," he says. "Any time you feel like taking a refreshing dip, let me know."

Our driver throttles down the motor so he can speak to us from the back. "This is Horn Creek Rapid coming up," he announces. "It's a big one. I want everyone low in the boat. Hold on tight." Somebody in the group stops him before he throttles up again. "What's it rated?" she asks. The guy grins broadly and leans a little closer. "Well, it's not too technical," he begins, "it's rated about an eight or a nine." He winks conspiratorially at his partner: "But we rate it a 10 on the Fun Scale." No one knows what to make of this oblique answer, but we all scrunch down into the raft as he guns the motor.

We soon learn that our boatmen use two systems for classifying rapids. Officially, rapids in the western United States are rated on a scale from 1 to 10, with 10 being the most powerful. Typically, anything above a 7 gets classified by most boatmen as "Big Water," especially if the rapid is peppered with dangerous obstacles, such as boulders, sandbars and snagged rafts. But our boatmen also make reference to a Fun Scale, which appears to be a classification for rapids that are high on water volume but low on obstacles. These offer enough of a margin for error that boatmen will play their rafts heavily through the waves for the shear pleasure of an exhilarating ride. As you might imagine, whenever a boatman runs a rapid that rates high on his Fun Scale, everyone but him gets wet.

A stiff foreboding wind blows up as we near Horn Creek Rapid. We will soon discover that this is common, as turbulent water makes for turbulent air flows in the canyon. Though I have plenty of time to do so, I don't get a good look at the rapid going in; I'm too busy shuffling my feet and hands around for a better grip. One of the guides had said something about not letting your feet slide down between the pontoons when gaps appear—something about compound fractures. Another said not to let yourself get tangled up in any lines—a sure way to drown. There are shouts of "Hang on!" and

"Here we go!" just as people do at the top of a roller coaster, and suddenly the boat dives forward at what seems like a 30- or 40-degree angle. I look up in time to see a silver wall of water just 6 feet away and closing fast. It blasts us like a hundred angry fire hoses, pumping meltwater from God's own ice chest. I take it square in the face.

An eight or a nine, he'd said, but a 10 on the Fun Scale.

We were expecting that the water would feel refreshing after the long hike in the desert. We were wrong. I tell Carolyn that I think this is going to be a vacation of extremes; we're either going to be too hot or too cold, but rarely comfortable. She just hugs her knees and gives me a look that says, "This was your idea."

After Horn Creek Rapid, our driver invites us to start taking turns "riding the horns." The horns are the front ends of the two long pontoons strapped to the sides of the raft—the nose cones, if you will. One is expected to sit astride them like mounting a horse; there are two rope handles to sit between and hold onto. There's just one rule when riding the horn: Dive into big waves headfirst. If you're sitting up when a big standing wave hits, it will more than likely sweep you right off the boat.

I pegged one guy as a macho dude right from the start, and he immediately slides himself out onto one of the horns. I decline the invitation. My male ego wants to get out there and prove itself, but I figure I've got five whole days in which to die; what's the hurry? For now, I'll just watch.

The next rapid is a small one, but the driver purposely hits it hard to give us a wild ride. The guy on the horn takes a good shot from the wave, but he's too cool to admit it. With false bravado, he challenges the driver to do better. Instead, the driver calls him back into the boat, saying "Maybe later. Right now we've got another big one coming up, and I want everybody low in the boat again." We quickly comply.

Again, the wind whips up and gives away the upcoming rapid before it comes into view. This time, I nestle in early so I can carefully watch the lead boat run the rapid ahead of us. Just in front of that boat I can see a discernible horizon line running all the way across the river. Occasionally, white froth leaps up from behind the line like solar flares in the corona. When the lead boat reaches the line, it tips forward dramatically, then vanishes instantly below the horizon. I'm stunned. Not even the crew of the Santa Maria could have imagined such an abrupt fall over the edge of the earth. When we reach the calm water at the bottom of the rapid, the adrenaline shuts down and everybody starts shivering—and I mean shivering uncontrollably, which includes the loud chattering of teeth. People start pointing at each others' quaking limbs and laughing, but even the pointing fingers are quivering.

The driver, still dry and cozy in the back, slows the engine again and stops Macho Man, who is once more climbing out onto the horn. "Crystal Raid ahead," he announces. "There are only two Class 10's on the river, and this is one of them. Kind of technical, too." He smiles broadly. "Guess I don't need to tell you to hang on."

"Jesus Christ!" says Carolyn, who has been dreading the Class 10's for weeks. "We're there already!" She's had Crystal Rapid and Lava Falls on her mind ever since I showed her my pocket river guide.

In near panic, we tear into our rain gear. We're more fearful of the river's temperature than its power. The driver slows the boat to accommodate the sudden flurry of activity, and we just manage to get ourselves together before we slam into Crystal. Cold fingers of ice water shoot up my pant legs and up my stomach beneath my raincoat. More icy fingers stretch slowly down my collar, neck and chest. I have to admit, it's exhilarating.

I take my first turn riding the horn on the second day of our trip, and I find it less satisfying than I thought it would be. I discover that just to stay on the damn thing I have to lean forward and kiss the pontoon every time we hit a big wave, and if I look up too soon after that, I often take a secondary wave right in the face. Still, it has become something of a rite of passage, so I shimmy out there whenever I can. A consensus is developing among everyone except the young bucks that the best ride to be had is in the "bathtub," the low area right in the very front of the raft. In the bathtub, a rider can keep his or her head up the whole time and see the action. Moreover, the bathtub is relatively safe, since the crashing waves hammer the bow-riders down into the boat, rather than sweeping them away as happens on the horns. The trade-off, of course, is that folks in the bathtub stay wet. Even the smallest waves manage to sneak up over the bow and rinse out the underwear of those riding there.

Our driver calls us in from the horns again as we approach Bedrock Rapid, which he says is very technical. "If I do it right, it won't seem like much," he continues, "but if I make a mistake, I want everybody low in the boat."

Bedrock Rapid is created by an enormous table rock—a flat slab of granite lying several feet under the river, over which the current slips, like a ski on snow. At the end of the table, however, is a sudden drop over a ledge, which creates a waterfall and a huge hole. Our boatman intends to stay off the table entirely by running the boat down a deeper channel that flows between the table on the left and a rocky cliff on the right. However, that channel, too, spills into the hole eventually, so the driver swings the boat around almost backward so that the motor's propellers are facing into the rapid, driving us away from the malevolently sucking hole.

Something goes wrong in the execution, though, and the raft slides gracefully and unceremoniously out over the middle of the table. There's nothing to do now but hold on. We go over the ledge sideways, the most common position for a boat about to flip. The raft flexes mightily. Straps stretch; rubber groans. The boat feels like it's coming apart—like it's going over the falls in pieces. First, the right pontoon drops away from under my feet; then we follow it over the edge in slow motion. We crash down hard and splash through a few small waves to calm water. I look back at the driver, who has an astonished look on his face. Then he flashes his trademark grin and slaps his partner a high-five. I decide to stay off the horn for a while.

Late that evening, as Carolyn and I lie on our cots watching the stars, conversation turns to our boatmen. They're young and intelligent men, well traveled, and most of them slowly pursuing degrees of one kind or another. They're a bit roguish, too. Some are ski instructors during the winter, but most of them seem to drift around during the off season, taking odd jobs here and there between excursions to the Southern Hemisphere.

I try to romanticize them by portraying them as river pirates. Take the driver of our boat, for instance: Between rapids, he lounges contentedly in the back of the boat on a beach chair beneath the shade of a large Molson's patio umbrella, which I'm sure he "liberated" one drunken evening from an unsuspecting sidewalk cafe.

I've seen the other members of our crew bartering ruthlessly with other river men for various foodstuffs and better brands of beer and soda. One evening, a guide from another company got drunk and convinced his partner, a buxom and sturdy woman, equally intoxicated, to pierce his ear on the spot. Other tales of inebriation include one about a guide who passed out and was then put to bed by his buddies, who spread peanut butter on his lips. Allegedly, a ringtail cat (kind of a cross between a raccoon and Pepe Le Peux) soon plopped down on his chest and "kissed" him until the peanut butter was gone.

Such stories, of course, are impossible to verify. They're always accompanied by the usual verbal affidavits and solemn swearings to the existence of photographic evidence, but the photos, not surprisingly, are never at hand. Few activities are as characteristic of river men as the telling of tall tales, and our boatmen are no exception.

They like to remain aloof, but they also enjoy spinning yarns just this side of the believable; and they really like to keep us guessing about what lies ahead, especially with regard to tomorrow's encounter with Lava Falls.

Lava Falls has been on everyone's mind from the outset. We were able to repress it during the early days of the trip, but as our encounter with it draws nearer, it comes up more and more frequently in conversation, eventually becoming the focus of our attention. The river men have contributed their share of hype, too, reminding us that Lava Falls is still waiting out there, whenever we've spoken too enthusiastically about a big rapid already under our belts.

As whitewater rapids go, Lava Falls is a notorious celebrity. It's widely acknowledged as the granddaddy of all rapids on the continent. Among Colorado river men, it goes uncontested as the most powerful navigable stretch of whitewater in the United States. We expect to run it a little before noon today.

Everyone is a little tense as we board the boats after breakfast, laughing much too easily at jokes that barely even warrant acknowledgment. We can't help ourselves; we have the brittle humor of folks on the edge. Many of us have seen pictures of rafts, even big pontoon boats, flipping over like toys on the surging tongues of water in Lava Falls. There is a long stretch of flat water before we get there, so we use the opportunity to snap last-minute photos of each other—smiling, drinking sodas, catching rays. We joke cryptically about making arrangements for the survivors to send the pictures to the families and loved-ones of those who don't make it. A woman with a video camera swings it from face to face, and we recite our names and hometowns for the record. I ask if the boat has a "black box" recording device like airliners do, and everyone laughs much harder than the joke deserves.

The walls of the canyon turn black as we drive into the volcanic region. Long rectangular tubes of cooled lava hang in great corrugated sheets above and beside us, blanketing the canyon walls like burnt plastic. We reach Vulcan's Anvil at around 10 a.m. It's an enormous chunk of lava that has broken away from the cliffs above and entrenched itself well out into the river. It looks like it could be 200 feet tall and about half that wide in diameter. It stands like a grim and silent gatekeeper almost exactly one mile upstream of Lava Falls, a monument to the damned. I half expect to find Dante's inscription on it, advising us to abandon hope as we enter.

One of our boatmen passes out pennies as we go by the Anvil and tells us that it's considered good luck among river men to land a coin on one of the Anvil's many narrow ledges. It reminds me of a cheap carnival game, but I catch everyone else's giddy enthusiasm and soon find myself jockeying for a good throwing position. In the past, I've been tossed out of rafts in the middle of Class III and IV rapids (eastern scale), and at times, I've thought I might not live to tell the tale. What could it hurt to have a little extra luck going into a Class 10? As our boat drifts rapidly in and out of range of Vulcan's Anvil, pennies rain down on it, and more nervous laughter fills the air. Not one to fool around, I pitch a dime. It falls short by about 6 inches and plops helplessly into the water. One quick flash of silver, then nothing. I stare for a long time at the spot where it disappeared. Carolyn pats me on the shoulder.

We take a few more pictures and make a few more bad jokes, then our driver gets our undivided attention by throttling down the motor. We look downstream but can't see the telltale horizon line. Nor do we feel the expected increase in the breeze. We look back at our driver, puzzled. "Listen," he says, shutting off the motor completely.

At first, nothing. Just the regular slapping of tiny wavelets against the raft. We shift positions, cocking our heads, leaning forward. "Shhhh," we tell ourselves.

Then the eyebrows lift in recognition, and some of us shudder visibly. The sound is faint but unmistakable, like a thousand people whispering together at the end of a long, echoing corridor. A waterfall! The sound alone triggers primitive survival instincts. I feel myself wanting to move to the back of the boat, wanting to move away from the sound. Even in this controlled situation, there's something very disconcerting about being pulled swiftly and inexorably toward that sound. If I hadn't already been told that we're going to stop and scout the rapid before running it, I'd probably be negotiating with the driver right now to put the motor in reverse. Then again, I probably wouldn't. I'd just drift silently and manfully along with the crowd, being too much of a coward to run away.

In no time, the menacing sound of the river and the stories we've heard combine in our heads to give us all mental pictures of an incredible and even supernatural torrent ahead. By the time the first angry white foam at the head of Lava Falls comes into view, the rapid has transmuted from an inanimate object into a living, willful thing. It has taken on mythical proportions, becoming a horror, a fury, a monstrous beast from ancient legends, resentful of our trifling imposition. By the time we are close enough to have its demonic rage thunder in our ears, our imaginations have completely gotten away from us.

It is no longer Lava Falls; it is Charybdis.

Six or eight empty boats of different styles and sizes cling to the black embankment on the right side of the river. It is apparent that no one runs Lava Falls without scouting it first. We tie off here, too, and scramble up a path worn in the lava to a perch some 50 feet above the river where a number of boatmen have gathered. We are told we will take turns running the rapid. The trip leader's boat will go first while the rest of us watch and photograph it from here. Then, as we go through, folks on the other boat will watch and photograph us from below. Everyone quickly exchanges cameras with people from the other boat.

Far below me, Lava Falls looks a little disappointing. Granted, it is a seething, swirling, surging stretch of frothy whitewater. But it appears to be only about a 100 yards long, and it doesn't seem to possess the impressive holes and standing waves we've been encountering on some of the lesser rapids. Perhaps it's just an illusion of perspective; maybe those particular features simply aren't visible from above. On the other hand, this might be a different kind of rapid all together, presenting greater challenges than mere holes and standing waves can offer. The boatmen are certainly behaving that way. They crowd together in small packs, but they do not speak. Most stand reverently at the edge of the path, arms folded across their chests, eyes fixed on the churning spectacle below. A few have taken seats right on the edge of the path, legs dangling carelessly over the cliff, watching the river in a kind of absent meditation. Despite the fact that they're all looking at Lava Falls, I don't get the feeling that they're studying it very carefully. In fact, they don't really seem to be scouting the rapid; they seem to be paying it homage.

While most of us are busy learning the idiosyncrasies of other people's cameras, I notice our trip leader shaking hands and exchanging solemn words with the driver of my boat. These guys have been hyping Lava Falls for several days now, but I don't think this is part of the show; I think they're genuinely wishing each other a safe trip, and I think they've chosen this moment because they believe we're not watching. But I'm watching. I'm not missing a thing. I decided early this morning that I was going to ride the horn through this rapid if they'll let me, and I'm on the lookout for any piece of information that might cause me to reconsider. In truth, I don't really want to ride the horn; the bathtub would be a much more enjoyable location, not to mention a safer one. Still, I have many friends back home who will want to know where I was on the raft when I challenged Lava Falls, and I can't stand the thought of telling them that I played it safe.

The trip leader assembles his party and leads them back down the path, leaving my group to fiddle with our new cameras and to contemplate our destinies. We also start negotiating for positions on the raft. There's some haggling over the bathtub and the left pontoon, but no one argues with me over the right pontoon.

It seems like an eternity before the other boat finally comes into view. Suddenly, the whole scene has new perspective. The 30-foot pontoon boat seems to shrink to half its size as it approaches the tempest. Our friends below look like puppets on a toy raft. They fall into the rapid and almost disappear in it, popping up from time to time like a submarine breaking to the surface of a rough sea. Their course takes them dangerously close to huge, jagged rocks on the right side of the channel. I pick right up on the fact that no one is riding the right pontoon. My pontoon. In a few seconds, they spring clear of the rapid and drift into calm water, swinging the boat around proudly to face us.

Cheers ring out from the boat below and from us above. Then our driver quickly assembles us and starts leading us down the path to the boat. "I don't think anybody rode the right pontoon," I tell Carolyn urgently, getting no response. She's absorbed in keeping her footing on the rough terrain. I shift my attention to Macho Man, who called dibs on the left pontoon. "I didn't see anybody on the right pontoon," I tell him.

"Didn't notice," he says obtusely. "Great ride, though, eh?"

"Yeah...great," I say, wondering if I can expect a straight answer on this subject from either of our two boatmen.

When we get to the raft, I take my place on the right horn and look back expectantly at the driver, thinking he'll suggest I move to another location. He doesn't seem to notice me. The other boatman is busy locking things down, and it takes me a while to get his attention. "Nobody on that boat rode the right horn," I tell him. No response. "Is there a reason for that?"

He looks up from his work and stares downstream for a moment. "Well, we are going to have to steer pretty close to those rocks over there on the right," he finally admits, "so if it looks like you're going to hit 'em, you'll want to jump back into the boat." He goes immediately back to work. Carolyn laughs a little at my predicament. I tell her she's a big help.

I keep staring at the boatman until he gets the idea that I'm still very uncomfortable. As he slips into his life jacket, he assures me that he'll shout out to me to jump into the boat if there's any serious danger ahead. I look for a place into which I can jump, but every last crack and crevice is filled with a body. "There's room over here," says the guy on the other horn, but I'll be damned if I'm going to hang on behind him like a girl on the back of a motorcycle. With renewed conviction, if not foolhardy pride, I swivel my hips and scrunch down tight on the right pontoon, wrapping my legs around it like Slim Pickens riding the H-bomb in *Dr. Strangelove*. I just hope I'm not riding to a similar fate.

On the flat water approach to the rapid, I lean forward a couple of times in preparation for diving into the waves. Like a pilot running a preliminary systems check, I grip and regrip the rope handles, pulling hard to test their strength. I feel a little foolish sitting so far out on the front of the boat, leaning into the wind. It occurs to me that to the people on the cliffs above, I must look something like a hood ornament.

Dropping into the rapid, we skirt just to the right of a huge hole in the center of the channel and ride out on a short tongue of semismooth water with raging rapids on either side. As we pass the hole, it assumes immense proportions; water pours into it at such tremendous volume that it appears to be swallowing the entire river. The hole is formed by a long, powerful waterfall that wasn't apparent from above.

We quickly run out of smooth tongue and dive into the agitated waters below. I duck in anticipation of an approaching wave, but we bounce over it instead of going through it. The rocks on the right are too damn closed—inches away—but I can't afford to let go in an attempt to jump into the boat. The raft twists and flexes madly as it crashes into waves of irregular size, and the pontoon bucks beneath me like an insane bronco. I find that with all the bouncing up and down and side to side, I can't hold my position securely on the horn. A big standing wave appears out of nowhere; I duck just in time, but it still knocks me back several inches, breaking over my head and shoulders like a ceramic vase full of ice water. I try to shake the water off my face since I can't let go of the ropes long enough to wipe my eyes, but smaller waves keep splashing up and blinding me. Not able to see what's ahead, I dare not raise up too far and risk being swept overboard by a big one. I sneak only enough peeks to assure myself that we're not getting any closer to the rocks. Needless to say, from that point on I don't see very much of Lava Falls. It stands out in my memory more like a rodeo than a rapid.

When we reach calm water, we punch our fists into the air in unison and let out a victory whoop. Our sister boat responds in kind. Carolyn is beaming. She chose a spot just to the right of the bathtub, and now she's wishing she'd been right in front. "It was like a roller coaster!" she says exuberantly, wearing a familiar grin that says, "Can we do it again?"

Our boat pulls alongside the other one for a short time so that we can exchange cameras again, trade stories and watch some other boats tackle Lava Falls. During our celebration, a number of people from the other boat congratulate me on having had the courage to ride the right horn. I'm confused, but I try not to let on. Eventually, one of them informs me that the trip leader wouldn't let anyone on their boat ride the right horn; he thought it was much too dangerous.

I look at my two boatmen, my two "professionals." One is casually cleaning his fingernails; the other is rubbing his feet with a pumice stone. "River pirates," I tell Carolyn, "plain and simple."

Ferocious Encounters with Norwegian Lemmings

By Frank Krajcovic

The real silliness started at about 4 p.m., with me trying to cook a spaghetti dinner on a Zip Stove Sierra Light gizmo that works pretty well, but works best at an altitude where you can find wood or something to burn in it. This was not the case. It looked like it would be a tepid dinner at best (I had brought a few twigs with me); but then a spectacular rain cloud appeared with an arm pointing at me like Uncle Sam telling me I was wanted immediately for the Norwegian Navy, and the thought of even a lukewarm dinner seemed a bit far-fetched.

Yeah, it rained. I was walking in one of the most glorious landscapes in the world, with glaciers, fjords, mountains and more waterfalls per square inch than any place on the planet, all within view simultaneously.

Actually, it was a lot prettier when you could see it, which was no longer possible because the rain was thick, and with it came a cloud that swept over the area I was walking on. Except for those times when I was walking on precarious-looking snow bridges or around dangerous-looking holes—but I didn't want to think about that. Nor, for that matter, did I want to think about the lightning, which was doing its best to brighten this gloomy day.

Prior to the storm, many of my thoughts had revolved around lemmings and their brash personalities. It hadn't been my original intent, it's just that lemmings have a way of insisting that you interact with them. These chipmunk-sized rodents with Napoleonic complexes stand outside their holes as you go by and curse you. They talk about your mother. They let you know that under ordinary circumstances they would think nothing of grabbing you by the ankle, flinging you to the ground and ripping out your liver to use for pate. Fortunately for you, though, their kids just had a meal. Still you had best be on your way in case the in-laws came over because they never seemed to get their fill of good food.

I waded a little farther and came upon the last sight I expected to see in this wind and rain—a tent. The tent was not faring too well. Two guys were repeatedly coming out and trying to repair and reposition their tattered shelter. They looked so miserable that I thought they might have lost their women to a pack of wild lemmings.

I kept on walking, wondering to myself why these guys had taken issue with the almost universally accepted wisdom that it is easier to keep warm by moving than by pitching your tent in an icy river. It was then that I came upon another tent a-flutter. It was a drab-colored monstrosity that looked like it could hold a small circus or almost all of Rush Limbaugh's ego.

When I got close, it became obvious that the inhabitants were singing Christmas carols in order to keep their spirits up. But when they got to the line, "Donner and Blitzen," I held in check my desire to make their acquaintance. Lonely mountain pass, haggard, hungry looking people, lots of snow, Donner; I decided not to tarry.

Eventually, though, all good things must end. The trail took a sharp left and went downhill just below the glacier. The wind died down. The air got warmer. The rain let up. The sun came out. Children started skipping around with baskets of flowers singing, "The hills are alive with the sound of music." This was beginning to get insipid, I thought, but soon the sound of children's voices were drowned out by the sound of my friends, the lemmings.

They were poking their heads out of the ground and were feistier than ever. It was like I was wearing the colors of a rival lemming gang from the other side of the mountain. They were giving me a pitiless verbal lashing until I came upon the brilliant strategy of saying that I was a Jehovah's Witness and would they like to talk for a while. Then they seemed to remember that they were supposed to be cleaning the basement or fixing the furnace and went back inside and left me in peace.

Writing Home

By Charles Straughan

No shit! There I was, hopelessly lost deep in the uninhabited vastness of a West Virginia wilderness. I had no food, no water and a swirling snowstorm was bearing down on me. I despaired of ever seeing home and hearth again.

My predicament had begun with a phone call from my father three days before. The old man wanted me to accompany him on one last hunting trip before he cashed in his chips. I knew that this would be our last father-son hurrah, and I wanted the memory of it to be like one of those warm, fuzzy stories that are always happening to other people.

My wife thought the whole idea was insane, but agreed to let me go if I promised to let her know exactly where our camp was located. If I didn't make it back, she wanted to produce my body right away for insurance purposes rather than waiting seven years to have me declared legally dead. She's very sentimental about things like that.

I left at dawn the next day for the 200-mile drive to a nameless crossroads town where I found Dad waiting impatiently. I loaded my camping gear into his battered old Jeep and off we went, two adventurers anxious to pit our mountaineering skills against the worst that Mother Nature could throw at us. We bounced and lurched over rocky ridges and plunging valleys for the rest of the day, stopping at dusk only because the ancient Jeep simple was outmatched by the trackless terrain all about us. Leaving me to set up camp, the old man strapped on his illegal deer spotlight and disappeared into the woods. He hadn't returned when I awoke the next morning, but that wasn't unusual for him. He would show up eventually, as he always did. But I was beginning to worry because of his advancing age and some health problems that I hadn't noticed before.

About midmorning, it occurred to me that I should let my wife know where I was. But how? A quick search failed to produce even a pencil stub. I didn't have a single sheet of stationery. Even if I did have these things, there was no place to mail a letter—also assuming I had the necessary postage, which, of course, I did not.

Suddenly, I remembered just how out of touch with civilization I was. In this part of the wild and wonderful West Virginia, there are no telephones, no Western Union, no game wardens (none who survived, that is) and no forest rangers. But that's the beauty of the place. You aren't supposed to be connected with the outside world in the midst of all this solitude and isolation.

The day before, I had seen the remnants of an abandoned road which at one time led up to an old logging camp at the top of the mountain. Could there be anyone up there after all this time? More to the point, could I mail a letter from there? I had to give it a try. The search took a couple of hours, but I found what was left of the logging road and started for the summit which seemed to get higher and farther away with each step I took.

After two hours of steady plodding, I was exhausted. It was already midafternoon and I was fast approaching the point of no return. If I turned back now, would I find our camp before dark? Then I thought about Dad. Good Lord, what if he came looking for me and his heart gave out?

To make matters worse, the temperature was dropping rapidly. A late fall snowstorm was blowing up, and I was getting colder and wetter by the minute. I was on the gritty edge of panic but I decided to push on toward the mist-shrouded summit.

My resolve paid off. Another hour of trudging brought me to the top of the mountain and an abrupt change of luck. Dusk was settling in as I rounded the last run of the road. Hallelujah! I could see smoke slowly curling from the chimney of a log cabin. There was a faded General Merchandise sign over the door with U.S. Post Office below it in smaller print. Salvation was at hand.

I staggered the remaining few yards and literally fell through the front door of the ancient store to discover the howling wilderness had saved its biggest surprise until the very last. The only other person in the little establishment was the postmistress who was sorting mail. She was easily the most beautiful woman I had ever seen, a startling cross between Marilyn Monroe and Brigitte Bardot with long blonde hair, deep blue eyes and long curling eyelashes.

"Can I he'p you, honey?" she said in that soft taunting lilt typical of Southern women. Putting aside her postal duties she oozed toward me. It must have been the shock of seeing this gorgeous creature in this unimaginable place, but it took a moment before I could recover my voice. Finally, I croaked, "Uh...yes...do you keep stationery?"

A slight blush tinged her china doll cheeks. Her long eyelashes fluttered uncertainly for just an instant as she brought her hypnotic blue eyes closer to mine. Still smiling, she said, "Well, I do for the first minute or two, but after that I just go CRAZY!"

I suppose I should tell you that all this happened 12 years ago, and I haven't been off the mountain since. I guess my wife has collected the insurance by now. I have no idea what happened to Dad. We plan to go looking for him one of these days real soon, but being an assistant postmaster keeps me pretty busy, you know.

Wild Thing

By Terri Martin

She shot from the trailer, hooves clattering, nostrils flared and tail lashing with ill temper. The cowboy man who'd transported the horse, a rescued mustang, wore his arm in a sling and walked with a distinct limp. His cowboy hat had taken a pounding somewhere along the trail. He whipped the lead rope at me with a degree of disdain nearly equal to that of the pie-eyed mare straining at the other end. The flea-bitten gray switched her gnarled tail and pawed the dust with a cracked hoof which bore testimony of her years on the range. Though far from a specimen of equine excellence (in fact the mare's sire and dam may have been unaware of the consequences of inbreeding), she had an athletic aura—lean and sinewy. The eye held a hungry, haunted look. Untamed at the least, wild, more likely. The rolling eyes seemed to question who will break whom.

"Hello, Wild Thing," I said.

The cowboy man spat an amber stream of tobacco juice at my feet.

"Good luck, Girlie," he said. "You'll be gettin' my bill for the damages, including the doctor's bill."

He gimped to his truck, pulled himself in with his good arm and fled in a spray of dust and gravel.

With the reluctant assistance of a half dozen curious onlookers, we maneuvered Wild Thing into her box stall. A foot of fluffy pine shavings littered the floor. Bright, sweet hay sat in her rack and sparkling clear water concluded the accoutrements painstakingly put in place prior to the horse's much anticipated arrival.

Her appreciation, if it existed, was subtle. Perhaps the confinement of the box stall was against her nature. When all possible avenues of escape had been exhausted—climbing, digging, kicking, etc., Wild Thing began circling the stall. When one direction became monotonous, she reversed and continued her dizzying rampage.

Soon the pine shavings banked the sides of the stall and a trench scarred the dirt floor thereunder.

The group of onlookers had grown, one of whom offered me a nip from his flask. Though only 10 a.m., it seemed a neat sip of brandy would perhaps relieve my building anxiety.

Indeed, the brandy cleared my muddled brain. Whatever was I thinking, putting a wild mustang in a stall? Wild Thing had progressed from the circular pacing to a modified rearing action, limited by her cramped quarters. Another moderate pull from the flask numbed my discomfort and further clarified my thinking. I suggested that we escort Wild Thing to more suitable environs. Perhaps the wide open spaces of a pasture with green grass and trees would make her settle in.

Surrounded by a herd of humans, Wild Thing submitted to the transfer. Indeed, she flew from her stall as if propelled by a cannon blast and we were only marginally in control during the brief but intense transition. She was funneled through the gate into the pasture, the lead rope removed from her halter. Wild Thing bucked violently, emitting a rude expulsion of air on the upswing, before thundering off across the rolling pasture.

"Now there's a happy horse," I said inanely and took a generous swig from the flask.

Wild Thing barely slowed before she sailed over the pasture fence and galloped off into the noonday sun. We stood a moment, mouths agape, unbelieving of the aerial display we had just witnessed. After a brief interlude, I gathered my wits and raced off after her, the purloined flask bumping against my thigh. The others never left the pasture gate and began the mumblings and mutterings of people trying to squirm out of an obligation. When chasing down a wild mustang who is on course for parts unknown, one finds out who her real friend are. On that particular morning, I was to learn that I had none.

Surely Wild Thing was not intent on finding her way back to the Southwest, since that would be a distance of several thousand miles. More likely, I hoped she would decide to set up housekeeping prior to reaching the green expanses of a freeway median. Visions of mayhem danced through my head until pushed out by a substantial intake of brandy.

I was mildly winded after my sprint to the fence that Wild Thing had negotiated with such ease. It was of wire mesh construction, so I could not squeeze through the fence itself. There was a strand of electrified wire strung along the top which made going over impractical. I took another swallow of liquid fortification and began some serious mulling. Basically one option remained, and that was to go under the fence. How unfortunate, I mulled, that we had had so much rain as of late, though the soft moveable terrain did make the squeeze easier. I emerged on the outside of the pasture noticeably heavier from an accumulation of mud, and felt it necessary to lighten my load, if only by an ounce or two. Wishing I had worn hiking rather than riding boots (obviously designed to slowly and systematically amputate each foot via the Achilles tendon), I pursued my wayward quadruped with resolve.

After cresting a hundred hills, crossing numerous dales and fording a swollen stream, I caught sight of the object of my wanderings. Wild Thing, the picture of contentment, was happily cropping meadow grass, her expression bordering on bovine. She eyed my approach, swiveling an ear like an antenna. As bucolic as the scene was, I knew that I couldn't leave the horse to her own devices. She must return to my care, submit to my gentle training, adapt to the domestic life or be destined for a European stew pot.

I did some more mulling, enhanced by my dwindling supply of brandy. Rivulets of sweat formed in the creases of my forehead and puddled in the corners of my mouth. Other glands produced feeder streams of perspiration along my neck, shoulders and armpits. These smallish lines of moisture joined at the backbone forming a river which churned into whitewater along my vertebrae. The horse appeared as dry as the Sahara.

How unfortunate that my long journey had taken in excess of three hours (middle age had slowed me some) and it was midafternoon. The prospect of trekking on foot back over hill and dale wearing boots ill designed for walking while leading a reluctant horse did not inspire me. However, if I were to travel atop Wild Thing, at a smart trot, I calculated that we could reach the stable well before dark.

I had saved one last swig for that moment. Though a lesser environmentally conscientious person would have thrust the empty flask into the shrubbery, I, a strong supporter of low-impact mustang tracking, tucked the empty vessel in my pocket. With firm conviction, I strode toward the mare, clutching the lead rope that had come the journey with me.

Wild Thing did not run away, nay, she chose a more subtle evasion. I would move a step toward, she would move a step away, making herself always out of reach. Once, as if to torment me, she allowed me to touch her. Sensing the right moment, she flung herself away just as I grabbed for the halter. This exasperating game continued for what seemed hours, and I was painfully aware that our journey back to the stable would have to be at a steady canter to beat the darkness. Already, the first hints of a waning day played along the ridges. To heighten my misery, it was becoming clear that the final vestiges of alcohol were percolating through my system, undoubtedly taxing my liver and certainly filling my bladder. I was on the cusp of sobriety.

I determined that I would have to engage my wits. What I needed was a horse treat—an apple or a carrot. My eyes scanned the terrain only to find what you would expect—rock, dirt, trees, grass and a candy wrapper. Without much hope, I pulled up a handful of grass and offered it to Wild Thing. It was absurd, really. She had acres of grass at her disposal. Why would she be interested in a few blades offered by a sullied human hand?

Why, indeed? I was amazed to find the leathery lips reaching, neck stretched for the offering. Her lips strained toward the grass which was just out of range. She moved a micromillimeter closer, and I, a plan grinding in my mind, inched farther away.

Again, she tried to close the gap, and I enlarged it. We continued this way, progressing perhaps a foot, until I sensed a frustration on the horse's part. At that point, I let her have the grass, but quickly pulled up another handful and held it just out of her reach as before. This method continued to work and we slowly made progress of perhaps 10 or 15 feet in the next half hour. I realized that, at such a torpid pace, not only would darkness fall that night but the darkness of many nights to come before we arrived at the stable.

While I was allowing Wild Thing to chew perhaps the hundredth handful of grass, I engaged in ruminations of my own. Our grass-luring activity reminded me of something involving a carrot and a stick. Essentially I was dangling a carrot on a stick in front of the horse to entice movement. If only I could fashion such a device, then I could dangle the carrot, tangible or intangible, in front of the horse and, with me astride, we would gallop briskly back to the stable.

I pulled a lace from my riding boot and tied it to the end of a sturdy stick. When I bent to pull some grass, my empty flask fell from my pocket. Curious, Wild Thing nosed the strange object and tentatively sniffed the flask neck. A tongue slithered from between lips and began working the exterior. I snatched the bottle and jammed it in my pocket. She pressed her muzzle into my pocket. I backed up a few steps, afraid she would tear my jacket. She followed. I executed various evasive moves to flee her advances, only to have my every step duplicated. There was certainly no further problem in approaching the horse. On the contrary, her antics caused me concern that I would be trampled for a drop of brandy. It seemed the mare would climb any mountain and ford any stream to satisfy her newfound lust. She couldn't, however, climb a tree and that was where I found myself, with pine needles exploring unmentionable parts of my anatomy. I still clutched my ridiculous stick and lace invention while I watched the horse mill around the base of the tree.

I can only attribute my sluggish thinking to the fact that I was becoming painfully sober and unable to shake the feeling of doom that encroached upon me like the darkness. Of course, the solution was so simple. A horse, whose brain resembled a lima bean, was trying to communicate an answer to our predicament and I, complicating the situation beyond necessity, could not see the forest for the trees, so to speak.

I fought the tremor in my hands as I secured the flask to the lace. Then, with one more or less swift movement, I dropped from my perch onto Wild Thing's back and jutted the dangling flask in front of her. I felt her back stiffen and her neck arched into a question mark. The flask had, for the moment, lost its appeal. Neither of us moved, digesting the significance of the moment. We continued in this non-mobile state for perhaps 20 seconds, each awaiting the other's move. Since I was the party presumed to be in charge (after all, it was I on her back—at least for the moment), I tentatively suggested forward movement via a gentle yet firm nudge in her ribs. This failed to produce forward movement but did cause Wild Thing to snake her neck around to explore the source of the offensive rib nudging. Much to my good fortune, she whacked her nose on the dangling flask. Her ears pricked forward with interest.

It started with one step, then another and another. Next came a brisk trot, the flask bobbing just out of her reach. Undaunted, Wild Thing broke into a canter which escalated into a collected gallop. Soon we were thundering through the rolling terrain full out, leaping streams and fallen timber, barely slowing for branches which tore my clothes and ripped the flesh from my left cheek. No matter! We were mobile! While clutching the tangled mane for security, I implemented a rustic but effective method of steering. If I needed the horse to go right or left, I simply swiveled my "carrot" in the desired direction. To stop, I lifted it above Wild Thing's head and she would screech to a halt, look around and sniff the air in confusion. Drop it down and off we'd go. The miles melted beneath us and just as the last trickle of daylight faded from the horizon, we came upon the pasture fence. With no urging whatsoever, Wild Thing jumped the fence. Onward we flew toward the gate where, in the remnants of daylight, I could see the gaping mouths of my fair-weather friends who I'd left standing there a millennium ago.

I whipped the "carrot" out of Wild Thing's vision just before reaching the gate and we came to a sliding halt, spraying dirt, to my satisfaction, on everybody. I hopped off and stretched the kinks out of my back.

My non-friends rioted around me, talking simultaneously, inquiring of my adventure. From the corner of my eye, I saw—no, it couldn't be! Yes, I was certain. It was Mike Wallace! He strode toward me, the *60 Minutes* film crew trailing behind. He pressed a microphone into my face, spewing questions at me like SCUD missiles. I hadn't seen him so excited since the Desert Storm thing.

"How did you do it?" he shouted. "How, in just a few hours, did you manage to tame a wild mustang?"

Sometime earlier, I had slid my stick/flask mechanism behind my back. Wild Thing was nibbling at it, creating a picture of docility. My mouth opened and words, stupid words, fell out.

"I, ah...it's all in my book, um..."

"You have a book?" Wallace enthused. "What's the name? Who's your publisher? Where can we buy it?"

"Um, well, it's not in print right now, I..."

"What! Some idiotic publisher has allowed a book, written by a phenomenal horse trainer like yourself, to go out of print?"

"Well, not exactly, you see, it hasn't been in print yet."

Wallace shook his head in disbelief. "It's criminal, the way these publishers and editors operate. Where's the manuscript?"

"Um, in the house."

Oddly, everybody swiveled their heads to look at the house some 20 yards away.

"So nobody's bought it yet?" inquired Wallace.

"No, sir."

"I can guarantee my publisher will want it on his desk by tomorrow morning. Can you have it there?"

"Um, yeah—sure," I said. More stupid words.

"Excellent. I will see to it personally that your book—what's it called?"

"Um—er, Wild Thing," I stammered.

Wallace laughed and shouted, "I love it!" He gave me a hearty pat on the back, and he and his film crew clambered back to the van.

I dribbled a few drops of brandy, requisitioned from the tack room first-aid cabinet, into Wild Thing's water bucket and deposited her into her stall. With great weariness and throbbing head, I trudged into the house, climbed the stairs and entered my room. I moved to my computer and booted it up.

Wild Thing, I began.

The Mountain Man (99.9% True)

By Rick Ruffin

Mount Pugh stabs skyward, about a two-hour drive from Seattle by Range Rover. Not quite as sinister as its dark neighbor to the north, Sloan Peak, a veritable dagger of a mountain, Pugh is nonetheless a respectable and lofty goal, set in a sea of tumultuous rock and ice. It's one of many Cascade peaks that look downright intimidating, yet aren't. There's a tourist route all the way to the top. For hardy tourists, I might add.

My friend, Tom, and I decided to climb it in spring, when snow cover would make it more than just a scramble. We loaded ice axes, a rope and a bunch of other crap in his jeep, and took off.

The next morning found us hiking up the trail, and in a couple of hours, we had reached the lake at the bottom of the peak. Tom's blister was about the size and color of the "Tomato that Ate Cleveland," so he took off his socks to lance and moleskin it. That's when we saw the Mountain Man. No shit, there he was.

He was standing alone, hands in pockets, staring up at the peak. He had on cotton trousers, red suspenders advertising a logging company, and a cotton shirt open to solar plexus level. He wore Frank Shorter vintage running shoes and wrapped around his waist was the only other piece of synthetic equipment on his body—a 4mm piece of faded perlon, supporting a pair of the most God-awful, ancient, hand-forged crampons yours truly had ever seen. Tom just looked at me and chuckled. I chuckled back, but not in jest. More like in awe.

"Yup, my Pappy gave me them," the Mountain Man drawled to us. "They're exactly nah-tee years old."

"And you wearing them on your sneakers????" Tom and I said in unison, our eyes wide in amazement.

"Yup. Haven't had a problem yet. I use this here li'l piece of rope to tie 'em on," he said, showing us the faded piece of perlon. "And if I get going too fast," he said, brandishing a trowel, "I'll just stick this here trowel into the side of the mountain, snow, I guess, and that'd slow me down."

Sheesh! Tom and I both thought at the same time. THIS GUY HAS A LOT OF HEART.

We started up the trail, the trowel guy, Tom and I. He told us he lived just down the road and he'd just started hiking. With the logging industry shut down and such, he needed the exercise. He'd always thought about climbing Mount Pugh, and well, now here he was. The Mountain Man went on to tell us about his friend who took a house cat to the summit of this very same peak—"jes follered him up the trail"—but as for himself, well, he wasn't really sure where he'd end up today. "Out for a stroll," was what he said.

Well, as soon as we hit the snow, our friend pulled out a pair of sunglasses only a narc would wear, put them on and strolled right away from us. We plodded along in vain, trying to keep up in our mountain boots and ice axes, but by the time we reached Stujack Pass with the North Cascades unfolded beneath our eyes, he was a little speck tooling up the summit ridge.

That's when we ran into the climbing party. They were from a large, Seattle-based outdoors organization, up here for a "scrambling course." They had warm clothes, Gore-Tex, this, that, ropes, all sorts of shiny hardware hanging off their belts, altimeters, compasses, energy bars, ice screws, maps, ascenders, everything short of the kitchen sink, which I immediately started searching for, knowing it had to be somewhere.

"We're not with him," I said, as we approached them, pointing to the Mountain Man, who was disappearing into the summit clouds like a Yeti.

"He's crazy," one of the group exclaimed, with a genuine look of concern on his face.

"There's a lot to be said for simplicity," I answered.

"But he doesn't have warm clothes, or anything!!" the others chimed in.

"No, he doesn't," I said, "but something tells me he can get himself out of anything he gets into."

The air was about 40 degrees Fahrenheit with a light wind, warm enough for a man in cotton pants, cotton shirt and butt-ugly sunglasses sporting a trowel for self defense—if he kept moving. Only if he kept moving. And moving he was. The Mountain Man was on the summit. A tiny ant on the huge summit cornice of Mount Pugh.

The club climbers showed us where they'd turned back (one of them did make it). They had slapped an inclinometer on the slope and measured it to be about a 56-degree gradient. Too much for beginners, they said.

So, Tom and I did what we had come here to do and moved on. We ran into the Mountain Man at the catwalk just above the steep snow slope. We squeezed past him on the ledge, then watched him go down, heel first, plunge stepping neatly into the soft snow, trowel ever at the ready. He was down the crux section in no time, flashing it in tennis shoes and "nah-tee-year-old" crampons. Then he hurried down the ridge and dropped out of sight into Stujack Pass. Neither Tom nor I has seen nor heard of him ever since.

A century ago, John Muir, after running amok all over an Alaskan glacier, returned to the warm confines of his ship. Appearing, no doubt, like a wet rat, he was pitied by his fellow passengers. "Don't pity me," he cried, his ice-blue eyes full of missionary zeal. "For it is you whose souls starve in midst of abundance!"

Like Muir, the Mountain Man definitely marches to the beat of a different drummer. Or maybe we do. Maybe he is normal and it is we—Tom, myself, the mountaineering group—perhaps it is we who are different, out of touch.

Here was a man tuned in to a wavelength amazingly free of excess static and chatter. He relied on the wind for guidance, the gurgle of the stream for advice, the throaty "thump, thump, thump" of the grouse for comfort. He relished the marmot's shrill, solitary call. He carried no food, no canteen, no real abundance of "things," nor did he really need them. A trowel, rusty spikes "nah-tee" years old, and cheap sunglasses sufficed. And when he got thirsty, with his hands gently curved, he had all the water he could ever possibly use.

Wild Mules Underground

By Nick Devone

No shit! There I was—but buy me a drink and I'll tell you a better one—about the mules and why you shouldn't go out at night. But if a group of young fellows sporting business suits and motorcycle helmets come through the swinging doors, pretend you don't know me, drink your drink, and leave. The Chamber of Commerce here don't like me talking to tourists so they have their Junior Chamber of Commerce Jaycees keep an eye on me.

For me to tell about the mules, I first have to give a little history about the mines. In Colorado, there are lots of abandoned coal mines, specially under Canon City and its environs. Back when the mines were active, they were mined and scooped out in room-and-pillar fashion. This created caverns, lots and lots of them. In some of the mines, sloping shafts were dug down to 1,000 plus feet, and coal was scooped out at two levels. This created subterranean caverns, one above the other. For miles around, all these underground chambers from all these mines were connected by tunnel passages.

Now, I'm telling all this, not because I think you're interested in mining, but because of the mules. I have to explain about the mines so that I can then talk about the mules. There are mules down there in the abandoned mines under Canon City. Herds of wild mules live down in that underworld of caverns and tunnels.

Creation of all those caverns and tunnels took a long time. Most of the mines did not become worked out and abandoned till the late 1920s. A few lasted into the 1930s. The Royal Gorge Mine lasted the longest and did not shut down till 1946.

There are wet mines, and there are dry mines. To work a wet mine, pumps have to be used to keep the water out. When a wet mine is worked out, its pumps are turned off and it's abandoned, it fills up with water and stays full. The mines that were worked under Canon City and its environs were neither wet nor dry. They were supposed to be and should have been wet mines; all kinds of

143

water oozed, seeped, soaked, dripped, leaked and rain flooded in. They never flooded and no pumps were needed because of the Royal Gorge; and now that they're abandoned, they still never flood because of the Royal Gorge. There are fissures deep in the ground. The mines are deep, but the Royal Gorge is deeper and there are fissure in between. The water that gets into the mines escapes through the fissures, cascades down the Royal Gorge and flows away as part of the Arkansas River.

Not all the water. A lot of the water remains in the mines. Down in that underworld of caverns and tunnels, in that labyrinth of subterranean chambers and passages, there are pools and ponds and even some bogs, plus streams and rivulets. Herds of wild mules have to have water to drink.

Mushrooms grow down there, too. Herds of wild mules have to have something to eat. There are also toads down there, but the mules don't eat the toads because they're herbivorous—at least most of the time. But from out of the dead toads, mixed with other rot and decay, grow the mushrooms, and these mushrooms are both truffle-edible and jack-o-lantern luminescent. Yes *luminescent* mushrooms. They provide starlight down there. The mules have starlight to see by 24 hours a day.

Don't laugh. This is serious stuff. What I'm describing is the ecological system of an abandoned coal mine complex in which everything is interrelated and reciprocal and interperpetuating. The universe is a perpetual-motion-machine, so the ecology down there is one of everything perpetuating everything else. Caverns and tunnels and fissures and flood water and rot and toads and mushrooms and mules and mule fertilizing dung, all these are ecologically bound together.

No. I'm no ecologist or biologist or botanist. I'm no expert on mules or mushrooms or toads. But I know one who is. Or was. I don't know which. While you're here, don't wander out if you hear rumbling underground. I helped shut down the Royal Gorge Mine in 1946. I showed him where all the mines were located. No. I never went down into the caverns with him. Too old. And he never asked. But I read his notes.

Mushrooms don't need sunlight. They love cool damp darkness. They also love dung. Down in the caverns and tunnels, there's both. The mushrooms sprout and grow from out of the decay and rot not only from the dead toads and other stuff brought in by rain floods, but also from the decay and rot of mule dung droppings. Timewise the mushrooms came last in the ecological sequence of things. First, came the mules. Next, came the toads. Then years of mule dung droppings mixing in with a slush of dead toads and other crud. Last came the mushrooms.

The first mules were not wild mules. They were work mules used by the miners to pull their ore cars up through the tunnel passages to the surface. Lots of work mules were used; depending on the size of the mine, as many as 50, never less than 25. They lived out their lives below in the caverns and never saw daylight except for the minute it took at the end of each haul to dump the coal at the mine entrance. They were daylight-blind and kept their eyes closed at the mine entrance because daylight hurt. They were kept in corral-caverns. Bales of hay to feed them were brought down and stored in barn chambers. Loose hay, lots of it, got scattered and spread through the caverns and tunnels and became part of the decaying mix of toads and dung and other rot.

Mules are uglier than horses, but smarter, also stronger and more surefooted and durable. They're hybrids, the offspring result of asses copulating with horses. They come out as a mule when it's a jack (a male ass) impregnating a mare (a female horse). They come out as a hinny-mule when it's a stallion (a male horse) impregnating a jennet (a female ass). A mule is more like a horse, while a hinny-mule is more like an ass. Lots more mules are bred than hinny-mules. All mules and hinny-mules are sterile, but they have normal sexual drives. Once in a blue moon, a mule mare will be fertile and give birth. The scientists say it's because she has lost her jackass chromosomes and breeds like a pure horse, despite not looking like one.

Now, all this genetic stuff about their being hybrid and sterile is true for all other mules and hinny-mules, but not for those that roam the abandoned subterranean caverns and tunnels and chambers and passages deep under Canon City and its environs. No, no, I'm not going to claim that this came about, that sterile hybrid mules became fertile and self-perpetuating because of mutation caused by nuclear radioactivity or by some mysterious force from outer space. I'm not telling science fiction. There have never been any sightings of flying saucers over Canon City; so, no, the mules below are not a herd of strange creatures from outer space. Sure, the ground south of Canon City is a little contaminated with radioactive waste due to the uranium ore mill that operated there for more than 30 years. Sure, that contamination may have caused some of our bugs to become a little bit funny, but not the mules. They had already become fertile and self-engendering before the 1950s which was when that uranium mill began to operate. I told him about the bugs, but he wasn't interested in bugs. Only in the wild mules underground.

Sit back and listen. This drink and the next one are on me. Here's the explanation, and it's rational and scientific. Atavism. Throwback. Reversion back to the primitive. The Italian criminologist and psychiatrist Cesare Lombroso was right, back in 1876—maybe not right about criminals and the insane—but right about mules. The wild mules down below prove his theories correct. They are throwbacks to the tarpan, which is the prehistoric wild horse that roamed—and still roams—the steppes of Mongolia and northern China and the forefather of both the modern horse and the ass.

The tarpan is also known as Przhevalsky's Horse because it was the Russian explorer Nikolai Mikhailovich Przhevalsky who discovered the tarpan in 1883. And what does the tarpan look like? It has the combined characteristics of the ass and the modern horse, except that it looks less like either of them because it looks more like a mule, only uglier. And what does a mule look like? It has the combined characteristics of the ass and the modern horse, except that it looks less like either of them because it looks more like a tarpan, only not so ugly. And what do they look like, the wild mules which live in the abandoned mines under Canon City and which are fertile and can self-engender? They are uglier than regular hybrid mules. They look like tarpans.

And what caused this atavistic throwback of a subterranean mule reverting back to being (almost) a tarpan? Mushrooms! Yes. Mushrooms! A mushroom which has an affinity for growing out of dead toads and which can glow in the dark can surely cause a little atavism in mules. And this is specially so in mules which were smart enough to escape from their human masters and flee from the drudgery of pulling heavy ore cars. That's how it started. Mules are smart and patient and will work for you for 20 years, waiting for one opportunity to kick you and take off. Some of them did just that and hid out and learned to live in the maze of worked out and abandoned caverns and tunnels where the miners feared to follow because of crumbling pillars and the danger of cave-ins. Then the miners left for good, and the mules had the whole underworld to themselves.

I'm almost done. Only this—uh? Yes, I'm going to tell you who he is. Or was. I don't know which. He's missing. Both him and his notes. Makar Apollon Przhevalsky, the great-great grandson of Nikolai Mikhailovich Przhevalsky. I don't know if I should be mourning him or cursing him. He promised to put me in his book. Did the Chamber of Commerce pay him off? Did the Jaycees take him for a motorcycle ride? Or did the mules get him?

The mules are harmless most of the time. They've even learned to come out of the mines, but only at night because they can't stand the sun. They come out and night graze to supplement their diet of mushrooms. Like tarpans, they're browsers and like to eat shoots and twigs and leaves. But every once-in-a-blue-moon, there can be heard in Canon City and its environs the sound of rumbling deep in the earth. It's the mules stampeding madly through the subterranean caverns and tunnels. They stampede like this when they get drugged on the loco-mushrooms which sprout in their underworld every once-in-a-blue-moon. Go ahead and accuse me of telling monster tales. There are some who claim that on the night after the sound of rumbling, the mules emerge from the mines pink-eyed and foaming at the mouth and prowl the countryside as carnivorous meat-eaters. The Canon City Chamber of Commerce insists that this is nonsense and encourages citizens not to mention it. It's bad for tourism. Uh oh! Remember—you don't know me—drink your drink—and leave.

Adopt the Fetal Position

By Didier Couvelaire

The atmosphere in the narrow waiting room of the maternity ward filled with the anxious feeling of apprehension as families and friends awaited the birth of another relative. I peered at my brother-in-law's hands and noticed that his fingernails had completely vanished. Only puffed reddish fingers were left at the extremity of his thick hands. I glanced at my own hands, then meticulously probed the glossy white linoleum floor around the hard orange plastic chair to make sure that my nails hadn't fallen off inadvertently. When I noticed that not a single male in the waiting room had any nails left on his hands, I wondered then why no research had ever been conducted on this challenging phenomenon when male fingernails vanish while their natural owners wait in a maternity ward.

"You know, the doctor outlined the fetus for me on the tiny TV screen when we came for a medical checkup a month ago," my brother-in-law whispered to me. *Fetus, fetus,* I thought. Hearing this word brought make memories of a particularly long journey I had once taken.

The trip in question verified with unshakable certitude that keeping your body warm by simulating the fetal position has its limits. My friend, Luc, and I reached those limits during a memorable February night.

We looked at our gear scattered on the dark blue carpet of my apartment. "Two ski bags, two ski boots bags and two backpacks," recapitulated Luc, amused at his inborn expertise with arithmetic. It was already seven in the morning, and the red hand of the outside thermometer was locked on 10 degrees Fahrenheit.

"I hear a banging noise outside. Can you take a peek out the window to check if it's Bob?" I asked Luc, relieved to have told Bob to pick us up at 6 a.m. sharp.

"That's him standing on the brakes," laughed Luc. I was pleased to hear that Bob's natural driving ability on icy roads had improved along with his punctuality.

"OK, let's get the gear and go. The train won't wait for us," I declared. "We have to reach Isola before tonight."

"Hey, guys, I thought only the two of you were going," chastised Bob, staring at our scarce equipment. The wind started blowing.

"Help us put the stuff in your...uh, vehicle, will you, before we all freeze to death," I said. The trip to the train station was trouble free, except for a couple skids which Bob dealt with promptly and efficiently, describing to us the better performance features of his car while driving backward.

"Next time, Bob, try to get your windshield replaced before offering us a ride," I grunted, slapping Luc's blue face to clean the frozen snow and revive him. Fortunately, the train was late, too. We bought our tickets, and enjoyed the warm waiting room as the drops of melting ice ran down our clothes forming two puddles at our feet. I meditated about the ski race waiting for us the next day, 300 miles away in the Alpine ski resort of Isola. "I hope we'll be on time for our connecting train in Marseille," I told Luc.

"No problem," he replied, having regained his natural pigmentation. "We can always beg the ticket collector to contact the station and tell them to wait for us. The majority of the folks here have to take the same train as we do. They can't ignore 50 or so passengers."

As incredible as it sounds, Luc was right. The train was still waiting when we reached Marseille. We grabbed our equipment and proceeded to the other gate. As we ran in the station, the crowd, which probably knew about us being late, scattered in all directions. I now wonder, though, if they weren't running for their lives, hounded by two individuals launched at full speed and armed with ski bags. "OK, Didier, you can sleep for the next two hours," smiled Luc. "I lived in Nice, our next stop, for 10 years, and I know the station like the back of my hand. I'll wake you up."

Great, I thought, as I closed my eyes, putting my fate into Luc's hands. I was in the middle of an interesting dream starring exotic belly dancers, when I felt my body shaking furiously under the effect of an earthquake.

"Wake up, Didier, wake up," screamed Luc, deafening me on the spot. "We're in Nice, and the train's stopping only for five minutes." We gathered our stuff as fast as we could and landed on the gate.

"Ste Maxime, station of Ste Maxime," a suave voice announced in a state-of-the-art microphone.

"Open the door, open the door, Luuuucccc!" I exploded, running next to the departing train, trying not to step on my tongue. "I thought you knew this place," I accused as we tried to enter the compartment, trying not to maim innocent passengers.

"*Erare Humanum Est*," riposted Luc, displaying again his erudition in Latin.

"OK, you're right," I agreed. "Anybody can make a mistake. Next time do it when you're with someone who isn't me," I begged. We spent the rest of the trip reminding the other passengers every other minute to warn us at least 20 minutes before reaching Nice. Impressed by our athletic performance while running next to the train with our outfit, they didn't dare tell us how they felt about having to share such a restricted space with two peculiar individuals.

In Nice, we went to the information booth to inquire about the next bus leaving for Isola, our final destination. I could hear a gastric melody coming from our stomachs. Our last meal had been a light breakfast at 5 a.m., and now it was 6 p.m.

"We're looking for the bus station for Isola," I said to the woman standing behind the information booth.

"The station is located in the northern part of the city about 15 minutes from here without traffic, and the last bus leaves at 6:20," she answered. We started working on our fitness program again, as we ran fully loaded to the first cab.

"If we reach the bus station for Isola before 6:20," I told the driver, "there's a big tip for you." The dark-haired driver looked at his watch, exposing the blue tattoo of a snake on his muscular forearm.

"Fasten your seatbelts and close your eyes!" he screamed, his voice nearly drowned out by the roar of the engine.

The cab came to a halt in front of the bus as it was leaving the gate. "I didn't know you'd been a professional stock car racer," I said as I gave the driver his tip, trying unsuccessfully to stop my arm from shaking.

"I didn't know either," he said, smiling at the discovery of his new talent. Luc and I boarded the bus and sat in the antique seats.

"Another hour and we're in Isola," said Luc, his white face still disfigured by the fear of the previous ride.

"I didn't know you knew all those prayers."

"Me neither," Luc responded. The passengers stared at us as if we were two aliens. I wondered if any of them had previously ridden a bus with two pale men, their hair standing straight up on their heads.

The snow was falling heavily now, and I was curious how the driver was able to discern the road from the rest of the scenery which I myself could not. The bus started to skid at regular intervals, as well as emit some creaking noises. The driver, thinking about the safety of his passengers as well as his own, decided to pull over at the next rest area and call another bus to the rescue. The invisible hand, one more time, had brought us luck. The next rest area, unexpectedly, came with a sort of cafe judging from the rusty sign sitting above the door. We rushed inside the empty place, pushed by the unknown voices screaming inside our stomachs. "What can I get you?" the tall and slender man inquired.

"Foooooooodd," roared Luc, drooling uncontrollably on the counter.

"I'm sorry, guys, but we're out of sandwiches. I sold the last ones to a group of tourists. But, but...I have a salami and a loaf of bread in my bag," amended the trembling waiter, guessing that Luc was considering cannibalism.

"How much?" I asked, wrestling Luc and his 200 pounds of muscle down.

"You can have both for free if you promise to leave immediately," the clever man said. We left the store, carrying our precious cargo to safety. We tore apart the salami with our teeth and bare hands, allowing ourselves a rest only to breathe.

"Definitely the best salami I've ever had," trumpeted Luc, wiping away the grease dripping from his chin with his sleeve. The other passengers, unaccustomed to sharing such a limited space with two Neanderthals, were looking at each other, trying to guess who would be next on the menu. But they didn't have time to figure it out, as the rescue bus came to a stop next to ours. We changed buses and, after 30 minutes on the snowy road, reached the ski resort, exhausted but satiated.

After having satisfied basic needs with style and diligence, we focused on our next objective: locating a hotel room to rest. After five unsuccessful inquiries, we pushed the huge glass door of our last chance to sleep inside. The red spotless carpet reflected the rays of artificial light falling from several crystal and golden chandeliers.

"Hello, gentlemen!" smirked the tall man, stiffened in a dark blue three-piece suit. "How are you tonight?"

"How much for a room?" I diligently inquired after my bags had silently landed on the carpet. The polite man muttered a price.

"What?" I blabbered. After hearing the price, I realized why the well-groomed individual had called us gentlemen. Only gentlemen would be out of their minds to pay such a rate. I surrendered my credit card and took the key, suddenly aware of why it was the only hotel with empty rooms. While riding the elevator, I tried to figure out the number of months I would have to work in order to pay off my credit card. I giggled nervously.

"What's going on with you?" asked Luc. "Are you insane or what?"

"Do you think a lot of friends will come visit us in jail?" I coughed.

"Well, I think our lawyers will," Luc estimated. We crashed in the beds and slept heavily, at least Luc did, judging from the volume of his snoring.

The next day, as a blizzard was blowing the last heavy snow fall in every direction, Luc and I converged on the office building to get the latest news on the race.

"Hi, we're here for the race," I said to the large middle-aged man with a black baseball cap engraved with the red letters O-F-F-I-C-I-A-L. I was, one more time, amused by my natural ability to recognize an official at first sight, or maybe it was because he was alone in the room.

"The race?" he mumbled, a smile slicing his face. "You didn't receive the notice?"

"What notice?" I asked, vaguely remembering a letter sitting on my kitchen table with the acronym S.F. for Skiing Federation.

"The race has been canceled because of dangerous conditions," he explained, his eyebrows merging together in the middle of his forehead. I dove my hands in my pockets to look for a rope or sharp object. "I'm waiting here for any participants who would be so stup... heh, courageous enough to come despite the blizzard. So far, you're the first two," he added, obviously pleased to be of help.

We left, retreating to the nearest bar, ready to add some more charges to our bankruptcy case. After an hour or so, we left the bar relaxed, eager to look for any vehicle on its way to the nearest train station. The next bus was scheduled to depart in two hours, and despite our spontaneous attachment to the place, we decided to go home.

Luc, using his inborn gift as a negotiator, particularly when brandishing a handful of bank notes, found us a driver in less than a minute. The rusty blue vehicle owned by our driver resembled a Volkswagen van or at least what might have been one a century ago. We awarded the status of saint to our driver when he informed us that he was willing to give us a lift not only to Nice, but all the way to Marseille. He told us it didn't bother him at all to help two nice fellows in need of assistance. He added that he'd use the trip to buy himself a new truck with the money Luc had generously given him.

So we boarded the van, sitting in the back between dozens of pairs of skis and poles, thinking that our pudgy bearded driver was certainly an expert skier even if none of the bindings seemed to fit the same boot size.

Despite the raging storm that shook the antique Westfalia, the first hour of the trip seemed like a minute as Luc and I dozed, our heads pressed against the rusty walls. We had left the chaotic previous day behind and were on our way home.

TACTACTACTACTACTAC. The van started sliding and rattling. It seemed ready to fall apart.

"Sorry idi..., heh, guys, but we have a flat tire," sputtered the driver, pulling into a woodsy trail without a human soul in sight.

"What do you want us to do?" implored Luc, his teeth clicking like Spanish castanets.

"Just go for a little walk while I fix the tire. It won't take more than a couple of hours," the helpful driver replied.

"I would prefer to stay and watch you do the job. You must be an expert at fixing things," I coughed, peering at the odd cargo of tools inside the van. The friendly driver argued for a minute but finally permitted our presence at his side, either impressed by Luc's powerful appearance due to numerous layers of clothing or satisfied with his already impressive ski collection.

The tire changed, we headed for Marseille again. After another three hours, we got off at the train station and thanked our cordial driver for the instructive ride. I remembered later we were much obliged to him for sparing our lives as well.

While buying our tickets, we learned another piece of good news. The train we were going to board wasn't going all the way to our local station but would stop 40 miles down in the valley. With our congenital luck, we were convinced that we would have no problem finding another skillful driver who would help us deal with the remaining miles.

The trip was a formality, at least until we reached the terminus. Then, mysterious events began forming to converge into another sequence of overwhelming bad luck. A tormenting invisible force was testing our murderous instincts to discover our respective breaking points, the moment when complicated and logical organisms start behaving dangerously in total disrespect for other living creatures.

After getting off the train, we left our precious sport cargo in the station checkroom, then headed for the tiny village, ready for some liquid in the local bar. After consuming numerous glasses of the local green alcoholic beverage called génépi along with finger food, we returned to the station to pick up our stuff and start hitchhiking for the remaining miles.

It was already dark and freezing. We spotted a trucker hauling four trailers, each carrying a small sailboat. The truck driver, wearing a little black mustache and a heavy jacket, was skillfully involved in a routine security check, kicking the tires of the trailers with his black hard-toed boots. We knew right away that traveling with him would be a pleasure, having been seduced by his natural expertise at dealing with security matters. What we couldn't understand was the presence of four sailboats in the middle of a deserted mountain town with a temperature of zero Fahrenheit.

"Hey, how's it going?" I asked the driver. "By chance are you going in this direction?" I pointed with my finger.

"Yes. Do you guys need a ride?" asked the trucker.

"Thank you for the offer, sir," I responded. "We have some equipment to pick up at the train station. Can you wait for a minute?"

"No problem with that. You can put your stuff in one of the boats." We ran to the station, delighted by the offer. The station was filled with cold darkness, though, and a sign hanging from the inside doorknob read: **CLOSED**. Luc barked some explicit words about experimenting with the fine art of burglary but finally gave up, lacking both the technique and the desire to aggravate our case. I went back to the truck to explain our misfortune. We had to stay.

"Too bad, guys, but I have to go. Can't wait any longer." I thanked him for his patience and looked at my watch as the man left with his peculiar cargo. It was 2 a.m., and the next train would leave at 5 a.m.

After discussing the possibility of hunting for a hotel room in a ghost town, Luc unveiled, one more time, his sagacious gift at building logical reasoning. "If the train departs at five, the station will open at four to welcome the first anxious passengers. We just have to kill two hours and take a nap until the station opens," he plotted. "I've noticed some passenger cars parked on the other side of the station. We can always use one of them for a couple of hours." Seduced by the idea of entering a premise without an invitation as well as saving some money, we entered the car, groping through total darkness.

"Hey! Watch where you're going with your hands!" screamed Luc.

"Sorry, but it's charcoal dark in here."

We laid down on the long seats and prepared for winter survival. I discovered with amusement that the window of our compartment was frozen inside as I tried to detach my forefinger without becoming an unwilling skin donor.

"Hey, Luc. My feet and my hands are numb," I chattered.

"The best thing to do when the temperature is below zero is to adopt the fetal position. You curl up and preserve body heat," babbled Luc. I curled up as he had suggested, ready to experiment with anything to keep from freezing. As I started to hibernate, I heard a rhythmic clicking coming from the other seat.

"Luc," I asked, "do your hear that clicking?"

"Of course I do. It's my teeth."

"Didn't you adopt the position?" I inquired.

"I'm so twisted that I feel like a giant snail with its skull jammed between its femurs. It's too cold in here. How about if we walk a bit?" he mumbled, stretching his body while his bones cracked like kindling.

After pacing the town back and forth for the sixth time at supersonic speed, we headed for the station. It was open. We took possession of our beloved belongings and crashed on rows of plastic chairs, laying as comfortably as possible. When the train arrived, we had to disentangle our bodies from an accordion-like shape that perfectly matched the modern design of the plastic chairs. We returned to our local train station after a 48-hour trip, unharmed, sane but broke.

We had proved, at the peril of our lives, the limits of the fetal position.

Snapper

By Edward Lodi

I turned cannibal not long after the day I went turtle hunting in the Huckamuck Swamp.

You don't need any special equipment to catch a snapping turtle, except sensible clothing, a good pair of boots—and maybe some common sense. (I think that particular day I left most of mine at home.)

You've got to be cautious handling a snapper. Most ornery critter you're likely to run into, outside of a bull alligator. The only reason a snapper is less dangerous than a gator is because he moves so slow. Clumsy when he's crawling. But look out for those jaws!

He'll take your hand off lightning quick, if you're not careful. Grab hold of his tail, hold him out at arm's length—that's the only way to handle a snapper.

Once you've got your snapper, what you do is plunk him into an empty barrel. Metal or wooden, it makes no differences so long as there's been no chemicals in it. Set that barrel outside the kitchen door and toss all your garbage into it. Table scraps, vegetable peels, coffee grounds—the whole nine yards. Now, where's a snapper spend most of his time? Why, at the bottom of some scummy swamp hole buried in the mud.

Eat anything, a snapper will. Mostly fish and frogs. Snails and bugs, too, if need be. And ducks. They're hell on waterfowl. I even saw one kill a possum once—tore it all to heck.

A snapper fresh from the swamp has a musty taste. But fatten him for a month or two on garbage, and he's just as sweet and tender as chicken.

That snapper in the Huckamuck must've weighed 50 pounds. I was smacking my chops just thinking about all those steaks and stews. I'd have caught him then and there, if I hadn't gotten careless.

I spotted that son-of-a-gun sunning himself on a rotten log less than 20 feet from where I was standing. All that separated me from 50 pounds of good eating was a sump hole I mistook for a shallow pool. With all that green scum floating on top, I couldn't properly judge its depth. Lucky for me the hole was a mere 5 feet deep with muck and not quicksand for a bottom.

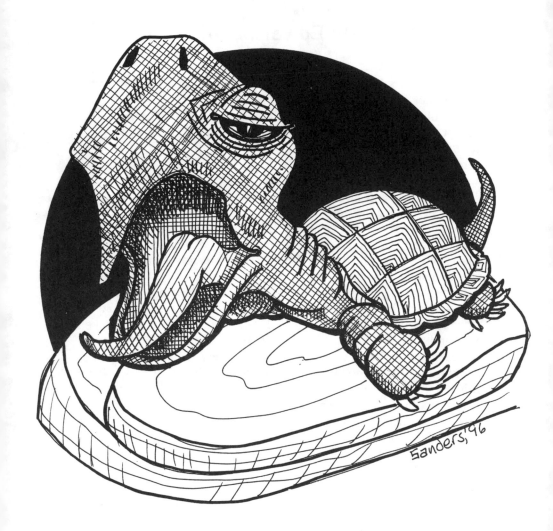

Sanders, '96

I knew I was in trouble when the water came up to my waist and I was still sinking. That muck took hold of my feet like a moray eel and wouldn't let go. The more I struggled to free myself, the deeper I sank, until the water was up to my chin whiskers. I thought I was a goner.

That's when I hit bottom. It wouldn't have been so bad spending the afternoon stuck in the mud in the middle of the Great Huckamuck, if it hadn't been for the mosquitoes. A good thing for me that the only part exposed to the elements was my face above the chin. As it was, the mosquitoes enjoyed a smorgasbord with me as the main course, crawling in and out of my nostrils and ear canals like spelunkers on holiday.

Now, I figured that despite suffering the death of a thousand bites, so to speak, I was in no real danger and would be rescued eventually. When I didn't return home by nightfall, my wife and kids would get worried and send out a search party. They'd find me and pull me out onto dry land.

And, that's exactly what happened, with one minor twist to the plot. Between getting stuck and getting rescued, the snapper awoke from his snooze. I'd never seen a turtle yawn, but when he awoke, those jaws opened so wide I could see down to his tonsils; he stretched out his feet, just like a lazy dog drowsing by the fireplace. Then, he scratched himself behind his ears and caught sight of me.

Now it's my theory he mistook me for a raccoon, what with my chin whiskers and all. When I saw him lumbering my way, the first thing that came to mind was my ears. I thought he'd attack them first, but no. He went directly for the nose. Bit it off clean with one swipe of those powerful jaws.

The thought of being eaten alive by a snapper had me so scared I hardly felt the pain that must have screamed from the place where my nose once resided. Fortunately, that snapper apparently found my flavor repulsive and I swear made a face like you would if you bit into something real unpleasant. Turned his nose into the air and paddled back to the log, burped a couple times and fell asleep.

Well, it wasn't more than a day or two before that rescue party found me. Not only had I not bled to death, I can honestly say "thanks" to that snapper. With this artificial nose the plastic surgeon fixed up for me, my allergies have cleared up and my wife tells me I no longer snore.

As for turning cannibal: I went back the next week and caught that varmint. Fattened him up in a barrel and had a barbecue.

I ate the fellow that ate my nose. I call that cannibalism. Don't you?

Outhouse Adventure

By Karen S. Minnich

This was my first camping trip with the entire family. Let me tell you right from the start that this was strictly my husband's idea. God knows, I'm not an outdoor person. My greatest fear in life is spiders. It doesn't matter, what shape, size or color they come in, I can't stand them.

But I didn't want to seem lacking in the eyes of my children, so I boldly went where others have gone.

The day started out as one of those that are etched in the mind forever. You know: blue sky, sunshine, caressing breezes, an absolutely perfect day.

The car and tag-along were packed to the fullest, and guess who had the honor of making sure everything was done? You guessed it. Me. How I wish there was another definition for mom and wife that hasn't been found yet. Something that would meet with my approval, instead of everyone else's.

We arrived at the campsite just as the sun was setting in the west. How convenient. We couldn't check out the outer perimeters of the site because there was only enough light left to set up the camper and start a fire for you-know-who to make supper.

With the evening meal behind us, we all got ready for bed. There was no porta-pot in our camper, and I asked my husband what was the standard procedure for going to the bathroom. He told me I had two choices: go behind the nearest bush, or go to the outhouse a quarter of a mile away. Naturally, neither met with my approval. I asked if he was sure that there was no other alternative. "No, dear, I'm sorry to disappoint you, but you're not at home."

I could see right then and there that things were not going to work out. I couldn't see myself squatting behind some bush with my bum exposed for some animal to mistake for a tasty morsel. My only recourse was to use the outhouse.

I asked my husband if he would kindly escort me to the facility.

"Come on, honey, I'll show you the way."

"I'll check on the kids, first, if you don't mind," I said.

"OK, then, let's get a move on."

Hand in hand we walked down the gravel path to the outhouse. As we went further, the light from the campfire became less and less. Finally, the only light we had to guide us was from the stars.

Directly off to the right I heard a faint rustling that became louder and louder with each step we took.

"What's that noise?" I whispered to my husband.

"It's only an animal," he whispered back.

OooK, I thought, Gene really should know what travels in the woods, since he is such a great outdoors man.

Suddenly, the hair on the back of my neck began to raise. I felt like something was breathing down it. It's just Gene, I said to myself, trying to be romantic, now that the kids were out of sight. I felt a moist tongue lick the side of my face. Punching Gene in the arm, I told him to lay off!

"What the hell did you punch me for?" he yelled.

"You know damn well how I hate to have my face licked. It reminds me of our Snooper."

"What do you mean, I licked your face? I didn't even touch you. Are you crazy?" he said.

"Well if you didn't touch me, who did?" I asked.

Just then I heard a definite growl directly behind us.

"Run, Karen, run like hell!" yelled Gene, as he grabbed my hand and dragged me along with him. We made it to the outhouse, ran inside and slammed the door closed.

In the time it took to suck in a deep breath, we felt something collide with the outhouse, followed by a loud howling, as if some creature was in pain.

Next came the unmistakable sound of claws raking down the wooden panels of the door, trying to gain admittance to our small shelter.

I didn't know what was worse: the fear of being mangled to death, or the overpowering stench emanating from the bowels of the outhouse.

Whatever was trying to break in was making headway as the flimsy panels began to give way with the onslaught of sheer strength.

"My God, Gene, what are we going to do?" I cried.

"There's only one way to save ourselves," stated Gene. "Down the hole you go, Hon."

"What the hell do you mean, down the hole? What hole?" I yelled.

"The one behind you."

"You expect me to go down that hole? No way, buddy!"

Groping in the dark, Gene lifted up the seat and reached for me. Grabbing me around the waist, he tried to get me into the hole. I had one thing going for me. I couldn't fit into the hole. For once in my life, I was very happy to be fat!

Finally, realizing that it was futile to keep trying, he gave up. I scooted over to the farthest corner and huddled in the dark to await our doom.

Perspiration was dripping off my forehead in beads and nausea was making its way up my throat as I heard the ominous splintering of wood. Well, here goes, I thought.

The next thing I remember, though, was something big and furry crawling its way up my arm. Well, you know what that was, one of my favorite things in the world. I let out a scream so loud that it deafened my husband and scared the shit out of whatever was trying to get in at us. Gene and I were greeted with silence after my scream faded into the night.

Whatever animal was after us, was long gone. Even today, it's probably still running. Never again will Gene reproach me about my big mouth.

Needless to say, I never did relieve myself in that old, smelly outhouse. I opted for going behind a bush after all. I looked at it this way, if anything went after my bum, I could always let out a mighty yell and scare the shit out of it, before it scared the shit out of me.

Returning to the campsite, I told my family we were leaving and to pull up the stakes. No one offered any resistance except our youngest, who said she had to use the outhouse before we left.

"No way, Kimberly! Use the bushes," my husband and I both yelled at the same time. The old outhouse would never see another one of us again.

The drive home was uneventful, except for a niggling itch on my rear end, that started right before daybreak. I really should have used tissues instead of those leaves, I thought to myself. One never knows.

Bull Ranch

By Lucile Bogue

No shit! There I was...with one of the Senator's fiercest bulls not six inches away, snorting fire down my heaving bosom! I stood straight in his path, frozen in terror. I could see myself entering the bull ring, a quivering lump of living hamburger, dangling on the horns of a raging bull.

But let's rewind to the beginning.

God! What a day that was! It started out great. The bright Mexican morning was hot and beautiful, busting with suppressed excitement. The busload of Whiteman School students fairly bounced with anticipation. We'd all been invited out to the Senator's bull ranch for the day, teachers included. Even I was all a-twitter, a middle-aged English teacher!

First thing the handsome old Senator did was to send the kids off God-only-knew-where to amuse themselves for a couple of hours, chaperoned by some of his trusty ranch hands. Then, he took the teachers into his private home for an early-morning shot of tequila, toasting me in particular with a deep, old worldly bow. I realized that he was quite taken with my black riding outfit, which fit me like a second skin.

Suddenly he disappeared but returned shortly, carrying a matador's cape. It was a gorgeous affair, heavy with embroidery in gold and brilliant silks. With great gallantry, he draped the cape around my shoulders with a flourish.

"Muchisima bella!" he exclaimed with satisfaction, but I knew he meant me, and not the cape.

With equal gallantry, Lowell Whiteman, the handsome headmaster, took his new black matador's hat from his own head and placed it on mine.

"Bravo!" the other teachers applauded. "Let's take a picture!"

So I was led out into the sun, where they all took turns shooting me in different poses. I'd never had so much attention in my entire life. I was floating on air—good, hot Mexican air. I was full of it.

After that, the Senator turned us over to his vaqueros, who had saddled up a herd of tough little Mexican ponies for an exciting ride out across the desert. This was the ranch where all the fierce fighting bulls for the ring in Mexico City were raised.

But the ride turned out to be far more exciting than my photo stint as a "model matador." Although I'd grown up on a horse on our cattle ranch in Colorado, this was a different kettle of Rocky Mountain oysters, I soon discovered. My pony was hard-mouthed, stubborn and downright mean. He bit and kicked at the other teachers' horses, and jerked the reins out of my grip every time I tried to curb him in.

The terrain was hellacious, nothing but black dry earth, punctuated at frequent intervals with sharp clumps of vicious yucca spines and outcroppings of jagged lava. What in the devil did the bulls eat? No wonder they were fierce! Could this grim diet have anything to do with my own bronco's ugly disposition?

Suddenly, without warning, my horse took off! Like a bat out of hell with his tail on fire, he shot out across the wasteland, managing somehow to dodge the yucca and the lava. How could I ever hope to cling to this wildly bucking beast? But cling I did, to the reins and the saddle horn, with the saddle pounding me cruelly at every jump. I stuck somehow, for my very life depended on it. If I landed on one of those lava spears...

All at once, Lowell was suddenly there beside me, his horse racing beside mine. He grabbed my bronco's bridle and jerked him to a halt. I knew Lowell was an expert horseman, but I hadn't expected this. He was truly magnificent.

The sparkle had left our riding adventure, though, and we returned to the corrals, with my horse following along in Lowell's stern grip, as meek as a mouse.

But our day was only beginning! There was the hearty barbecue on the patio of the hacienda. I preferred to stand for the feast, which I unfortunately barely tasted. I was too damned sore to sit.

Then came the bullfight. Or rather, several of them. We were taken to the small grandstand at the Senator's private bull ring, where his own picadors toughened the bulls up for their final fight to the death in the big ring in Mexico City. What we viewed was not the bloody slaughter of the big time, but only the preliminaries, the teasing of the animals, building up their rage and frustration with just the proper amount of torture.

The whole thing sickened me. Or was it my own tortured body that sickened me? It was all I could do to sit on the harsh wooden benches. I'd been pounded to a pulp from the waist down. But after all the warm graciousness the Senator had shown us, I had to be polite. At least for a short time.

But, thank God, I had an early escape planned! I had come in my own car so that I could leave in the middle of the show. My daughter Sharon was arriving back in San Miguel de Allende on the afternoon train from the States. Hallelujah! I had a legal getaway!

I crept down the stairs as stealthily as possible, under the cover of a wild burst of applause from the students, honoring a slick move by the poor bull. Like me, they pitied the animal. But then, they had never confronted one. Nor had I.

Carefully I swung open the heavy wooden door, hoping it wouldn't squeak.

No shit! There I stood, nose to nose, with one of the fiercest of the Senator's fighting bulls! I was frozen—paralyzed—staring into his fiery red eyes, his black nose snorting smoke and horror into my face. Slowly he lowered his head for the attack. For the second time that day, I faced sudden death. The sun glittered from the points of his cruel horns.

How I closed that gate so quickly, I'll never know. Just as I dropped the heavy bar into the slot, he struck! The whole grandstand shook with the impact.

But I was free. Jesus! What a day!

Once Bitten, Ask a Thai

By Mark Deem

The scream of tropical monkeys shattered the still of the jungle night, echoing through the canopy.

"Stop that screeching and hand me the Mekong!" Dave demanded, apparently unimpressed by my simian imitation. We were lounging luxuriously in the crooks and limbs of a huge jungle ficus, watching the moon and stars through the gaps in the canopy above us. Half of the bottle of Mekong (the finest rice whiskey one can buy for $3 American) had disappeared somewhere in the treetops, and Dave and I were feeling fine.

Our third week of wandering Southeast Asia found us in the jungles of Northeastern Thailand, looking for caves the guidebook swore were nearby. Our camp was spread out 30 feet below us, hidden in the dark by the thick veil of stringers dropping groundward from the tree limbs.

As the first mists of evening draped through the treetops and the Mekong warmth began to lose ground to the jungle chill, we headed down to camp. Swinging lower and lower from stringers and vines, Dave finally gave in and howled ape tunes at the moon.

Down in camp, we looked around at the intricate web of strings we had woven hours before to keep our mosquito net tubes strung taut over cheap backpacking hammocks. "Shoulda coughed up the cash for the jungle hammocks," Dave sighed, picturing the trapeze act we'd have to complete to get into bed.

"What we need is a camp fire!" I declared, beginning to root around in the piles of leaf litter covering the jungle floor with one hand, brandishing the Mekong with the other. I had a nice little pile of wood built up by the time Dave fished out the flashlight and joined me.

"Ow!" I yelped, dropping a log as a painful prick fought its way upstream against the Mekong from my hand to my brain. A few seconds later, my brain turned over the recent event and decided that some follow up was in order. "Dave, shine your light over here—I think I just got bit...."

Dave complied, and picturing more of the giant carpenter ants we'd seen around camp earlier, I kicked the log over. There, spotlighted center stage, pincers clicking, spiked tail flicking and legs working overtime to exit stage left, was the first scorpion I had ever seen. I looked at Dave. Dave looked at me. The scorpion headed for the hills. Then Dave uttered the two syllables hated most in outbacks the world over: "Oh, SHIT!"

I sobered up faster than a teenager looking at flashing lights in the mirror of Daddy's Buick and dove for the guidebook. Spiders, plants, snakes, muggers, Australians looking for a loan—the damn book had an illustrated section on every danger to be found in Thailand—except scorpions.

A strange tingling sensation was spreading through my fingers as I hurled the book at the nearest tree. Nervousness was quickly turning to panic when Dave remembered seeing a sign up the road that might have been a ranger station. I grabbed one of the dirt bikes we had rented the day before in Kanchananbury and kicked savagely at the innocent machine. Sweat poured down my face as the bike stubbornly refused to turn over. Years of kicking and cursing passed in the few moments it took me to realize that the fuel supply was turned off. The bike roared to life and nearly spun out of control as I jerked it toward the path, spraying dirt and leaves at Dave as he jabbered something about my not being in any shape to drive.

Dave caught up to me just as I was skidding to a stop in front of a crude wooden A-frame hut with an official looking plaque nailed to the door. I pounded the plaque until a light came on, and stepped back as a weary and frightened Thai woman opened the door. She fled back into the hut at the sight of the bug-eyed sweating idiot waving his hand at her at 3 o'clock in the morning, quickly replaced by an angry-looking husband.

The game of charades which followed would have been hilarious if my life hadn't depended on it. I stood in the ranger's doorway, frantically curling and flicking one finger like a scorpion's tail, sticking my index fingers in my mouth like Dracula's buck-toothed cousin, and pointing at my swelling hand. Dave stood over my shoulder trying to explain the situation in Thai from the now battered guidebook—which didn't have the Thai word for scorpion.

Just at the point when I was sure I would either lapse into toxic shock or get shot by the alarmed ranger, his face suddenly relaxed, his unfurrowed brow signaling comprehension. He nodded quickly, fluttering his hands to calm me down, then disappeared into the hut like a white rabbit through a hedge.

I slumped against a roof post, relieved that help was on the way. I pictured the primitive anti-venom kit the ranger was surely retrieving. I thought about the nearest hospital—a crudely tiled affair 120 kilometers away, down rough dirt-crusted roads. Visions of my convulsing body bouncing over those roads in the back of a battered Thai pickup truck swirled before me while I waited the lifetime it took the ranger to return.

He finally returned to the doorway. I rushed forward, my hand outstretched toward the instruments of my rescue. Relief turned to horror and confusion as the ranger brought forth the scorpion anti-venom kit—a little round tin the size of a quarter! A little pink tin with a picture on the lid of a monkey holding a seashell! As my jaw dropped and my brain short-circuited, the ranger removed the lid and applied something that smelled strangely like Ben-Gay to my numb, tingling, swollen hand—with a toothpick!

I turned woodenly to Dave, who shrugged, lifting his brow and hands in a gesture of confused surrender. I turned back to the ranger, mouth still agape, hand still outstretched. The ranger smiled, placed the tin and toothpick in my numb palm, flicked his hands in the universal sign of "shoo" and closed the door behind him. The light winked out, plunging us back into the dark of the jungle night.

"I guess it's not that serious," Dave said quietly, with his usual stoic understatement. He turned and headed for the cycles, leaving me alone in the dark with nothing to do but follow.

Back at camp I drained the last of the Mekong to still my jangled nerves. Thoroughly soused, one hand numb and useless, I turned to confront the rigging of the hammocks. Several minutes of wild thrashing, swinging, twisting and tangling ended with the inevitable. With a wild scream and a final flip, I spun upside down in the hammock and hit the ground, the sound of my mosquito net shredding filling the air.

Beaten and broken, soiled and sobbing, I crawled back into the twisted cords of my hammock. Pulling the remaining scraps of netting over me, picturing scorpion venom battling malaria in my bloodstream come morning, I drifted into sleep and dreamt of the virtues of a Club Med vacation.

Appendix
Author Biographies

Lucile Bogue

Lucile Bogue recently celebrated her 85th birthday and the story that placed in this year's contest will be appearing in her soon-to-be-published book, *Around The World In 80 Years...And Then Some!* As she puts it, "I've had so many adventures I can't let them go to waste!" Lucile has been a teacher on four continents and had a whale of a good time on every one. While adventuring around the world and working, she's been a constant writer as well, having ten books published, at least that many trying to find an editor, and a dozen or so in the incubator. "It's a great life," she says. "Wish it could go on forever!"

Ronald Bourret

Ronald Bourret spent ten happy years as a climbing bum in the western parts of the U.S., Canada and Europe. Now reformed and chained to a desk as a technical writer in the software industry, he is hoping to fall off the wagon soon. He lives in Seattle with his wife and partner in misadventure, Karin Gallagher. None of his heroes have ever been cowboys.

Bill Cross

Bill Cross is a writer and river runner living in Ashland, Oregon. He is a co-author, with Jim Cassady and Fryar Calhoun, of *Western Whitewater from the Rockies to the Pacific: A River Guide for Raft, Kayak, and Canoe*, which covers some 165 rivers in 11 western states. Bill's adventures and misadventures on western rivers have inspired articles for *Adventure West, Canoe & Kayak, Outdoor Family* and other publications, and he is a contributing editor for *Paddler Magazine*. He runs rivers with his wife and three children, and occasionally brings along an ancient springer spaniel for added challenge. Bill was also a finalist in last year's *No Shit There I Was...* writing contest.

Didier Couvelaire

Didier Couvelaire was born in Lyon, France and has been living in the U.S. for six years. He graduated from the University of Washington with a Bachelor of Arts in Journalism, working as a free-lance correspondent and teaching French in the Seattle area. He is a translator and co-editor for *The Poem & the World*, a series of international anthologies which publish the work of poets from Seattle sister cities. His poetry and stories have appeared in the *Licton Springs Review, Buffalo Bones and the National Library of Poetry*.

Mark Deem

With "Once Bitten...Ask a Thai", Mark Deem marks his second year with *No Shit There I Was...* His stories from last year's edition (*Slammed By the Salmon* and *The Maylay Melee*) have yet to rocket him to fame and fortune in the outdoor literary world, but Deem remains hopeful. When not kayaking, climbing, hiking, trekking, surfing, skiing or writing, he spends a lot of time looking for outdoor partners who will still answer their phones when he calls. Deem and his indestructible partner Dave have recently been blacklisted by every major life and casualty insurance company in the free world.

Nick Devone

Graybeard Nick Devone is a retired bleeding heart Social Worker, MSW, ACSW, now occupied in writing short stories of wry humor that are naughty but not salacious, impertinent but not offensive. His work has been rejected by the best editors in the country, but undaunted, he persists in his quest to prove that frivolity can also be literature.

Mike Ferrell

Mike Ferrell lives, works, and writes in Oregon, the torso of the Pacific Northwest—God's country to even the most agnostic. His poetry occasionally appears in literary journals, magazines and newspapers. He classifies himself as either an armchair adventurer or an adventurous sofa spud. He divides his time living on the edge of a cliff and cornice or couch and fireplace, trying to understand why the attraction of one kind of edge is so compelling from the perspective of the other.

Michael Hancock

When not sliding down mountains, running from killer bears, or challenging rivers, Michael and his wife Deedee can be found in Land O' Lakes, Florida. Michael is an engineer by trade because nobody will pay him to do the other things. Although a published photographer, this is his first published story.

Jonathan M. Karpoff

Jonathan is Professor of Finance at the University of Washington's Graduate School of Business. He serves as Managing Editor of the *Journal of Financial and Quantitative Analysis*. None of this, of course, has anything to do with stumbling around in the wilderness, something at which Jonathan truly is proficient. Devil's club is his constant outdoor companion. In the middle of the night, Jonathan steals time to write about, or make up, his adventures.

Lindsay S. Koehler

Lindsay is happy but embarrassed to tell her tale publicly, and swears it is true. She, Dan and Jim continue to have adventures (ask about the grapes-pretzels-and-gum sailing incident or the malfunctioning compasses canoe trip) in and around the wilds of northern New Jersey. (That's not supposed to be funny. Stop laughing. There are, too, wilds in NJ!) She has since been accused of killing a nesting pair of swans which lived until recently in a neighboring lake—but the autopsy revealed the culprit was "limp-neck disease." Honest. One of her (admittedly small) claims to fame is that she lives near the only retail outlet for Campmor (be jealous to make her feel good), where she found out about this contest. She works as a "community relations coordinator" at a humongous Barnes & Noble, where she gets to hang out with authors, speakers, and their ilk. By the time this is published, she and Dan hope to be living aboard their 28' sailboat, and someday they plan to chuck it all and sail south.

Frank J. Krajcovic

Frank J. Krajcovic is a high school english teacher and a ropes course instructor, a former stand-up comedian and a former coordinator of the Appalachian Long Distance Hikers Association. He is half owner of a cordwood and stone house that has lots of arches, a sauna, and no electricity or running water. The house is in rural Maine, which is only 700 miles from where he lives in Virginia. In the summer he can usually be found beneath a backpack. His trail name is "The Merry Slav."

Edward Lodi

Edward Lodi first ate snapping turtle when as a boy he worked on the cranberry bogs on Cape Cod. "The ditches were full of the plump reptiles; once you scraped off the leeches they weren't bad eating at all." But, tastes change. He is now a vegetarian and refuses to even wear turtle neck sweaters.

John Long

John Long's instructional books have made him a best seller in the outdoor industry, and his award-winning stories—known for taut action and psychological intensity—have been widely anthologized and translated into many languages. His current literary fiction has appeared in everything from *Granta* to *Readers Digest* , Of his twelve books, over 750,000 copies are currently in print. A legendary performer in rock climbing and adventuring, Long made the first one-day ascent of El Capitan, and the first free ascent of Wahington Column's East Face (both in Yosemite Valley), still considered the world's greatest free climb. Notable expeditions include: Baffin Island-North Pole; first coast-to-coast traverse of Borneo; discovery and exploration of the world's largest river cave (Gulf Province, Papua New Guinea); first descent, Angel Falls, Venezuela; and first land crossing of Indonesian New Guinea (Irian Jaya), said to be the most primitive region in the world. From the late '70's through the '80's, Long wrote for various network television shows. His novella, "Rogue's Babylon," was carved apart and reassembled in the Sylvester Stallone movie, *Cliffhanger.* One-eighth Comanche, Long has been deeply interested in all aspects of Native American culture for many years, a voyage of self-discovery that resulted in his recently published anthology of Indian folklore and legends, *Pale Moon* . Long, winner of first place in the *No Shit* contest for the last two years agreed (after being threatened with a darn good thrashing) not to enter this year. He did, however, comply with our wishes to offer a story for publication. Thanks John!

Terri Martin

Terri Martin wasn't born in the saddle, but allegedly her first word was horse. She began horseback riding at the age of five, a phase her parents hoped would soon pass. Several decades later, the phase has not passed and Martin still owns three of her quadruped friends. During her equine tenure, Martin has shown, been a riding instructor, pleasure ridden and fox hunted. In addition to her devotion to horses, Martin is an avid outdoorswoman who enjoys backpacking, hiking, camping and bird watching. She works as a legal assistant to support her habits and in her spare time has written magazine articles and yet to be discovered novels.

Karen S. Minnich

Karen S. Minnich has been writing short stories and poetry since 1972 . Her poetry has appeared in *American Poetry Anthology* and *Our Western World's Most Beautiful Poems*. Mrs. Minnich is the mother of four grown children, and lives with her husband, in a sylvan setting, at Beech Mountain Lakes, in Pennsylvania.

Rick Ruffin

Rick Ruffin is forever and hopelessly a mountaineer.

Rick Sanger

At press time, Rick Sanger was living in "Das Bus" (a turquoise, '58 Chevy school bus) in his most recent ploy to entertain his parents. Since his first visit to the Sierra, as a Boy Scout, he has been irreconcilably drawn to their magic. Twenty years later, he landed a job as a seasonal backcountry ranger in Kings Canyon National Park. He has made a career of avoiding careers and rationalizes this unwillingness to get a "real" job by maintaining that diverse experience freshens the psyche, nurtures wisdom and promotes humility. He has started Sangergy Press to publish his first children's book, *Are There Bears Here?*

Michael Shepherd

Michael Shepherd is a greehorn writer from San Lorenzo, California, who learned from last year's *No Shit* contest, to write this year's bio in the third person. His reckless spirit has gotten him beat-up by unbroken, barebacked quadrupeds, shot at, stabbed, and chased by helicopters. That's the short list. More recently, he's managed to get himself served a slice of humble pie by an adventurer/author of world renown (last year's contest winner)— it was a meal he ate with a sheepish grin. Despite all, he's been blessed with a larged, devoted family and has managed to squeeze in some fishing, skiing, hunting and motorcycling. His spirit remains strong, but his reck-lessness, thankfully, is finally being tempered by the accrual of hard-earned wisdom—and some very special young 'uns. He placed third in last year's contest and his writing has appeared in *Men's Fitness* and *Outlaw Biker*. He is currently imprisoned in Pelican Bay State Prison, where he writes and awaits freedom and a reunion with his family.

Peter Stapleton

Peter Stapleton is currently working for a large national law firm, keeping records and bravely handling his "serpent-phobia" even in the midst of hundreds of corporate attorneys. He recently accepted a transfer from Los Angeles to Chicago, where the closest structures to mountains have high-speed elevators and thick, secure windows. He also writes for and co-publishes a political humor zine, *American Saga*. But he doggedly pursues his day-job's responsibilities, hoping to one day quit writing altogether. He can be reached by e-mail at "scoob@xsite.net."

Charles Straughan

Charlie Straughan was born in Logan, West Virginia in 1928. He is now a retired trust banker living in Naples, Florida where getting lost is a lot more difficult—and less exciting—than in his youth. He has traded his hunting rifle for fishing gear and is no more successful afloat than he was afoot in the hills of his home.

Brian D. Whitmer

Brian D. Whitmer, 36, teaches history and social studies in Silver Spring, Maryland. As if his job isn't challenging enough, he spends his summers and holidays seeking adventure in the great outdoors. More often than not, he finds it. He likes to assure his students that even though he has been struck by lightning, shot at by banditos, and half-drowned by whitewater rapids, he still considers a wilderness expedition to be safer than driving the Washington Beltway. *Pirates* is the third story Brian has placed in the annual *No Shit* story-telling contests. He hopes that an upcoming trip to Central America will provide him with a story good enough to take first prize in next year's competition.

Marcus Woolf

Born in Huntsville, Alabama, Marcus Woolf resides in Southern California where he enjoys surfing, climbing, and trying to figure out just what the hell a double-tall, decaf, nonfat Latte is and why the locals are so high on drinking wheatgrass juice. Marcus received a BA in English and Journalism from the University of Alabama; and he will neither confirm nor deny that he was a U.S. Army journalist. He is currently an assistant editor of *Outdoor Retailer* magazine.

Judging Criteria

All stories published within this book were presented to the judges anonymously and were submitted in the same format and style in which the contestants submitted them to us (if we received a hard-to-read copy with sloppy editing, that is what went to the judges). The judges were asked to evaluate and score each story in two categories: Entertainment Value / Compelling Storyline and Professional Crafting / Writing Quality. Each category was awarded a point total between 1 and 50 with one being the least favorable and 50 representing writing perfection (no, no one earned a fifty, but yes, a few came close). Both scores were then totaled and each story was awarded an overall score somewhere between 2 and 100. I tallied the scores from each of the judges to arrive at each story's final score. I congratulate all the finalists and the top 22 finishers whose stories appear in this book.

The judging panel involved editors and publishers from the following magazines:

Canoe — Judy Harrison, publisher; David Harrison, editor-in-chief

Sports Traveler — Beth Howard, west coast editor

A very special thanks to all the judges from myself and ICS Books.

IT'S TIME FOR ANOTHER BOOK...and another writing contest!

It's an Annual *NO SHIT! THERE I WAS....*Writing Contest

Tall tales are the stuff legends are made of, the meat of glory and the marrow of adventure. Gathered around campfires or smoky watering holes that smell of beer and musty wood, adventurers the world over regale all who will listen in that time honored tradition of recounting unbelievable stories that more often than not begin with, "No shit! there I was...." Exaggeration within moderation is key. Humor is important. Elements of the unbelievable are a must.

Award-winning author and humorist Michael Hodgson and ICS Books are seeking your accounts of personal "No shit, there I was..." stories. Tell us your best *outdoor adventure* tale of glory relating to climbing, mountaineering, scuba diving, skiing, whitewater boating, mountain biking, hang gliding, adventure travel—the list is endless as long as it pertains to the outdoors (no urban assault or my dog ate the cat stories please). Stories that may put the author at personal risk of embarrassment or international incident (such as the imbibing of local intoxicants while traveling abroad and/or sex-related fables—nothing illegal that will get us all into trouble please) may be published under a pen name at the author's request. If your story is good enough, it may be published along with a select number of other top story entries in Michael Hodgson's and ICS Books' upcoming title, *No Shit! There I Was....?* If your story is really good, and we mean embellished with appropriate humor and bravado, combined with a touch of believable exaggeration, you may be awarded $2,500 as the winner of Michael Hodgson's and ICS Books' annual *No Shit! There I Was...* contest. Runner up wins $750. While this may not be the quickest path to fame and fortune, seeing your story in print sure as heck promises to be a lot of fun and who knows, Hollywood may seek the rights to your story—Nahhh!

Send two copies of your story in double-spaced, typewritten form enclosed with a signed copy an official entry form to ICS Books. One copy of your entry must be ready for judging with all author identifying marks removed and only the title of the work and page numbers at the top of each page. All entries must be received by December 1 each year for that year's contest. Winner and runner up of the contest will be announced August the following year during Outdoor Retailer's Summer Expo in Salt Lake City. All authors of stories selected for publication will receive an autographed copy of *No Shit! There I Was...* Submission of story for contest grants one time rights and permission to Michael Hodgson and ICS Books to publish your story in *No Shit! There I Was...* and subsequent promotional material with only byline attribution and no financial compensation. Contest is not open to ICS Books employees. Judges of the final round of the contest include a select panel of top magazine editors. Preliminary qualification judging to pare the field down to a final round of stories is performed by a select panel of professional guides, Michael Hodgson, and Tom Todd, publisher of ICS Books. Decision of the judges is final.

Of course, no one can enter without an entry form. To request your entry form, contest deadline information, contest manuscript entry style recommendations and information, and prize details, either call ICS Books at (219) 769-0585, Fax ICS at (219) 769-6085, or write ICS at 1370 East 86th Place, Merrillville, IN 46410.

STATEMENT REGARDING ACQUISITION OF RIGHTS

Author Michael Hodgson and ICS Books only seek to acquire 1st time rights for publication of contest entrant's stories in the *No Shit, There I Was!* anthology series. Any and all contest entrants may subsequently sell their stories to magazines, newspapers, or other publications at will. Previously published stories will also be considered. Any request for reprints from the book that involve a contestant's story will be referred directly to the contestant for negotiation.

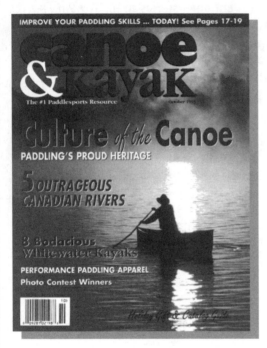

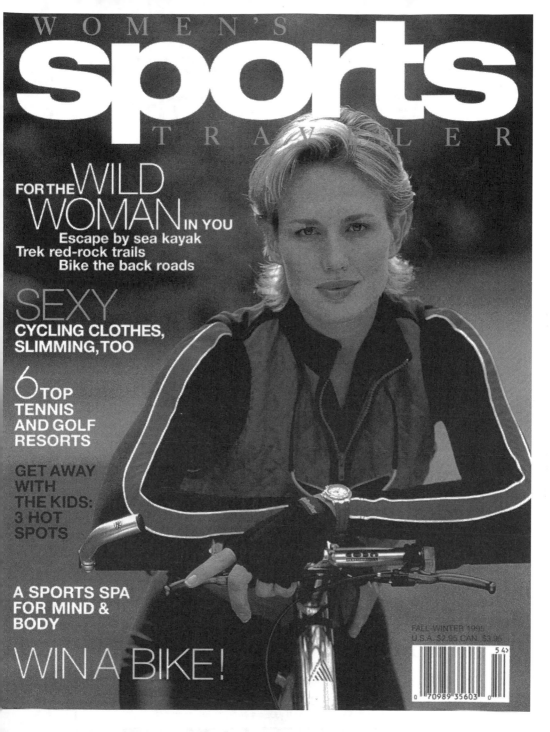

WOMEN'S

sports

TRAVELER

FOR THE WILD WOMAN IN YOU
Escape by sea kayak
Trek red-rock trails
Bike the back roads

SEXY
CYCLING CLOTHES,
SLIMMING, TOO

6 TOP
TENNIS
AND GOLF
RESORTS

GET AWAY
WITH
THE KIDS:
3 HOT
SPOTS

A SPORTS SPA
FOR MIND &
BODY

WIN A BIKE!

FALL-WINTER 1996
U.S.A. $2.95 CAN. $3.95

0 70989 35603 0

A Magazine for the Active Woman

FEATURING TRAVEL, OUTDOOR ADVENTURE, SPORTS, GEAR AND FASHION

To Subscribe Call: (212) 759-1357